Late Bloomer
It's not too late to Succeed!

Chad C. Betz

ISBN-13: 978-1717078476
ISBN-10: 1717078478

CreateSpace Independent Publishing Platform
North Charleston, South Carolina

Cover Art is based on Lens flare 34 by aloschafix

Author Photo by Alberto Torres

This book is dedicated to my family for the support and time they gave me as I wrote this book along with the friends, mentors, and coaches who advised me during the process.
~CCB

Table of Contents

Late Bloomer

Introduction

Late Bloomer

You are probably reading this book for the same reason I wrote it. You are wondering if you missed the boat and if your opportunities to reach your goals are behind you.

As I reviewed my career, both professional and personal I see that I have had accomplishments, but I am not where I wanted to be at this point in my life. I looked back at all the mistakes I made and the successes I have had and realized that it was time to make a decision.

I had to decide if I am just over the hill and ready to coast to the finish line or if I still had some fire in my belly and was willing to put in some extra work to achieve the goals I have yet to achieve.

I made the decision to push forward, to go out and work to achieve my goals. I can see that the path is not easy, but it will be exciting and satisfying. In the book, we will explore obstacles that I have encountered because they better illustrate what we need to overcome as late bloomers. We will also touch on some successes.

When you look back at your life, even if you feel that you have not achieved your goals, you will see that you have had successes. It is important to celebrate the successes and overcome the obstacles.

As you read this introduction, I hope that you feel the spark of hope that you too still have it in you to achieve your goals. You do not have to give up on what you want most and settle for what you have now.

The book is structured to:

1. See what this late bloomer thing is all about (chapters 1-2)
2. Demonstrate what do we need to do to set ourselves up as late bloomers (chapters 3-9)
3. Stick with the plan (chapters 10-11)

I hope you join me on this journey to achieving our goals and becoming Later Bloomers!

If you have questions when reading the book, go to www.latebloomerbook.com and submit them. I will be answering questions via YouTube so that we can share each other's experiences.

Chapter 1 – Are You a Late Bloomer?

It is never too late to be what you might have been.

George Eliot

The time for action is now. It's never too late to do something.

Antoine de Saint-Exupery

Late Bloomer

Where are you in your life journey? If you are like me, you have traveled pretty far down the path, but you do not feel like you have made the progress you expected. We based our success on all the examples we were given growing up. We needed to go to school, get a job, work hard and we would get to where we wanted to go. We started down the path and the faster we moved along the path, the more we started to be told that success is a young person's game. As we got more experienced, people celebrated youth and discounted experience.

Media constantly bombards us with lists. There are the 20 under twenty and the thirty under thirty. What about the 50 over 50? If you were to listen to these lists, you would start believing that if you were not a success by 25, your career, your life is over. Why is it that we focus so much on youth and forget about the experienced people? Not all of us will be a striking success at 25 or 30 or 35. We all make mistakes. Many of us have setbacks, and we do not always have the opportunities at the time we are ready for them.

Does this mean we are failures? If you take all of these lists to heart, you may think so. Through this book, I want to set the record straight. We all have challenges, and we are not necessarily ready to succeed when we are young. We may have developmental issues. We may be insecure. We may have obligations that keep us from reaching our goals. Does this mean we missed the boat? Did the door close to opportunities? No! It did not! Opportunities are everywhere. They may not be the opportunities we were expecting, and they may not come when we expect them, but they are there if we look hard enough.

We sometimes disregard our successes along the way and dwell on failures. Dwelling on failures can make us feel like we can't win. We need to celebrate our successes to help us believe in ourselves and believe that we can succeed as we move forward.

Opportunities are not all "once in a lifetime." There are opportunities all around us, and we need to go and seek them out. We need to do the work.

"Opportunity is missed by most people because it is dressed in overalls and looks like work." Thomas Edison

Because it is flashy and gains headlines, there has always been a focus on younger people. However, it is even more pronounced now. The dawn of the Millennial generation has increased the focus to the point of being a source of discouragement for the 40+ generation. As parents and grandparents, we have focused on our children and gave them ample opportunities to "win." The trophies for everyone theme has pushed itself to the forefront in adulthood as well. The focus has been on young people starting business and succeeding. It has perpetuated the myth that we need young people to energize companies. Young people can do it, but they are not the only ones. With proper preparation and focus older people can be just as, if not more, effective in energizing companies and being great leaders.

We don't all develop a strong experience base at the same rate. There are a few people who graduate from high school or college and are ready to start a business or run a company, but they are the exception, not the rule. It is not even that common. That is what makes them newsworthy. If success in youth were the norm, it would not make the news. Succeeding in life takes experiences, and we don't all have the same base of experiences.

My high school experience is a good example. My school was on the border of a struggling city and a well-off suburb. There were students with wealthy parents and students with struggling parents that did not want their kids to go to an inner-city school. The students were in the same environment. They had the same opportunities presented to them, but they did not have the same ability to take advantage of those opportunities. There were students who could not afford to take advantage of certain opportunities. Some students were distracted by things happening in their neighborhood. Some students had parents that did not have English as a first language. Even though the students were all presented with the same opportunities, their ability to take advantage of them were different.

There are also people who are just not mature enough. They fooled around and may not have known the opportunities presented to them or they had talents that were not applicable at the time or were not yet discovered. Schools put these people into the same box as people who were mature or who had a more conventional talent chain. The teachers tend to leave people with less conventional or yet to be discovered talents behind and focus on the easier, "in the box" students. The out of the box students do not experience the success the more mainstream students experience and can be discouraged to the point of not pursuing the talents they have. They could be left behind on the success train when they are younger. That can cause a pattern of failure in life that we need to convert into success with the right guidance and motivation.

Some people have developmental issues. They may struggle with reading or math or social skills. Many times, these students can be segregated even in class. This treatment can get them labeled as stupid or weird, and it makes it more difficult for them to integrate into the class as they get over their difficulties. The focus on core skills to succeed in school contributes to leaving many of those students behind. They get labeled as failures for not succeeding at tasks that most people never use in the working world. People forget that most people don't use calculus or even algebra on a daily basis so a student's difficulty in math should not prevent them from succeeding.

Early success and success in school does not necessarily equate to success in life, but we are led to believe that failure in school or early career leads to future failure. The people who love us propagate a lot of this. They try to protect us and encourage us to do better, but they end up perpetuating the myths that early success is the only success, or that staying in the middle is the safest place to be. They caution us not to take risks. They see our past failures and project failure in our future even though we learned our lessons from those failures. They want to protect us from getting hurt, so they caution us against anything they see as having the potential of getting us hurt. They do not take into account that the chances of gain are much higher than those of getting hurt.

"The No. 1 reason people fail in life is because they listen to their friends, family, and neighbors." Napoleon Hill

They tell us it is too risky to go for the new job or to move to a new city or to start your own business. They also look back on their experiences and end up giving bad advice. They don't mean to limit you. They are trying to help you.

There are times however where people are trying to hurt you. There are abusive relationships that leave people feeling stupid and unworthy of success. This relationship does not make a person a failure, but the relationship can plant a seed in their minds that put these people on the path for failure, making it more challenging for them to get back on the path to success. These situations can take time to get over and can make you miss out on opportunities and the "fast track" to success. When people do miss the fast track, they need to change their attitude, so they don't get discouraged while they are learning to succeed.

I see through my network of friends and colleagues as well as through the media that people believe that success has an expiration date. They feel that they have a certain chance and that if they miss that chance, they no longer have opportunities to succeed. This perceived lack of opportunity is a misconception, and it can lead people to give up on themselves. It is true that as I finish out my 40s that I need to work harder to maintain my energy than when I was in my

20s. I can't coast through life. I have to work to stay on top of my game.

Just because I need to work harder does not mean that I cannot succeed. Through movies and maybe the careers of our parents we saw that we work hard when we are young, then we are able to coast into management positions because we have "experience." If that were ever true, it is not true now. The environment we work in is vastly different, and we need to adapt to succeed.

Issues from this new environment include:

- Working in flat organizations that have fewer chances to get ahead.
- Having international outsourcing that reduces the size of domestic workforces dramatically.
- Work from home programs that isolate us from our peers and superiors, so we cannot properly showcase our skills.
- Being trained for one type of career that was obsolete before we even joined the workforce.
- Falling into the trap and feel that we can no longer get ahead if we are 40 or 50 or beyond.
- Having the wrong skill sets.
- Letting our bodies go to seed.
- Conflicting obligations.
- Having unbalanced lives combine with the fear of missing out.

These are all things that we can use as reasons why we should no longer try to get ahead. You'll notice I did not use the word excuse. These are not excuses. They are real, and they affect us every day. We need to account for them when we are planning our lives. In our later years, we have responsibilities that go beyond what we thought of as success when were younger. We need to define what we mean by success; we need to consciously pursue it and be flexible in how we get there.

Flexibility both physical and mental is crucial in being a late bloomer. Things are constantly changing, and you need to be able to take advantage of those changes not be overwhelmed by them. Whether it is technology or economic changes you need to stay on top of new challenges of all kinds. A belief "that's the way we always did it" is not a path to success. You will not get the results you want by doing the things you have always done. You need to adapt to the new environment if you want to succeed.

If you are going to make it to the next level, you need to change your game. Late blooming is just that. You are changing and opening yourself to new opportunities. You need to be flexible enough to change what you are doing to change your goals and to reach your goals. It can be harder when you are older. You may feel like you have been beating your head against the wall for years and years and you are tired. You want to rest and give up. Physical flexibility and fitness can overcome this feeling of distress.

When we get older, our bodies change. If you are overweight and stiff, it can be difficult to get around. You have less energy which changes your perspective. Being heavy also changes the way people look at you. People will tend to discount what you have to say. You also need to stay in shape and eat right so you can make it through the late nights and hard work that comes with success. Fitness gives you mojo, and you feel more powerful when you are fit and flexible. Remember, fitness does not mean becoming a fitness model. You don't have to be a bodybuilder or a marathon runner. Being able to tie your shoes without having to sit down is more useful than bench-pressing 300 pounds.

In everyday life, flexibility is more important than strength. We are more likely to have to bend down and pick something up than we are to have to move a heavy object. Flexibility helps us get into small cars and other tight spaces. When I was heavier, I had to hide my trouble getting out of a particularly small Uber. It was obvious I was having trouble and even more obvious that I was trying to hide it. Situations like that can be embarrassing. No one will bat an eye at you if you can't lift a heavy object but having trouble getting out of a car is a different matter.

We don't bounce back from long workdays, nights out or workouts as easy as we used to. We need to plan our days and manage our diets and activity to allow us to keep pace like we could when we were younger. My firsthand experience includes working out with strength training and having had trouble getting out of bed the next morning. My long commute exacerbated this fatigue. After being in the car for 1 ½ hours, I needed to take my time getting out of the car, and I felt old. When I work on my flexibility, my mobility is better, and I feel younger. To get there, I combine a mixture of strength and flexibility that allows me to feel younger, and I have the energy to keep pushing.

Being cognizant of what you eat is also very important. Junk food will slow you down and drain your energy. It may also put you in the bathroom rather than in an important impromptu meeting. Eating healthy will help you get you the energy you need.

We have been programmed since we were toddlers on how to see success. The need for success when we are starting out is reinforced from a young age. Sports are a good example. The teams and sports camps start when kids are really young, and those teams can be very competitive. There is the pressure that if the young kids don't participate in these teams and camps, they won't succeed when they are older.

We see the little kids at t-ball and in their football uniforms. I even saw a video online of kids' strength training. The pressure to succeed at a very young age can be overwhelming. My son decided that he wanted to wrestle in high school. When he started, he found he was playing catch up. Many of his teammates had been wrestling for years. Finding out you trail your peers is a point where many people get discouraged. They see that they are behind, and they quit. My son followed a different path and continued through and had a relatively successful run. Now that high school is over, many of the experienced kids quit, but my son has persevered with the fighting arts transitioning into Brazilian Jiu-Jitsu. He saw what he wanted and went for it. Even as a high schooler, he was a late bloomer for competitive wrestling. Catching up can seem like an even bigger obstacle when you are 40.

As a late bloomer, our choices drive us. When we are kids and even young adults, we are more driven by our surroundings. We are influenced by our friends and family and our circumstances as we have experiences that change, and we start to see new opportunities. We need to keep our energy up to accept those opportunities. As kids our parents guide us. When we are adults and need to make decisions without that guidance, we can tend to decide on doing nothing. That is the easiest thing to do. It is the path of least resistance.

When we do nothing, we lose opportunities. We need to learn to make choices for ourselves. After falling into the trap of least resistance, we will find ourselves at the whim of other people. Like a boat without a rudder, the tide will push us in the direction other people dictate. We will be helping other people achieve their goals and will be doing nothing to achieve our own goals. Remember when you are on that path, you may not be able to jump off of it. You will probably need to make incremental steps to get on the path that leads to your goals. If you work in a traditional work setting with a boss and a fixed set of tasks you may have limited choices on growth in that specific environment. You may need to address some things before you can get on a path that leads to your goals. Addressing these things means making some choices on how we treat ourselves including how active we are. Working in a sedentary workplace can drain our energy and make us feel lethargic. When you feel lethargic, you will not want to put in the work needed to make the changes to get you on a successful path.

Physical activity outside the workplace is a good way to keep your energy up. Exercise and sports will help you maintain the level of energy you need to get the job done. Our energy level is another area where age influences us. If we were not active when we are younger, we tend to get the "it's too late" attitude about sports and exercise. This is not true. It is never too late to start getting active. Not only will you get the energy you will feel a lot better about yourself. You may not be able to run a marathon from the get-go, but you can gradually work up to your potential. Not everyone is going to be an Olympic sprinter, but everyone can find an activity that they enjoy doing. It can be softball, golf, walking in the woods or something more aggressive like running or martial arts. You may need to try a bunch of things to find what you like. It is just important to be active

Late blooming is a mindset. We need to move beyond the common belief that we cannot have great accomplishments once we reach a certain age. We most often consider the idea of a glass ceiling when talking about women in the jobs marketplace and the difficulties they can experience. People who had not succeeded when they were young can have a self-imposed glass ceiling above them.

Whereas some people are held down, potential late bloomers tend to hold themselves down. I have seen pictures of horses standing still because they are tied to a chair. This chair is an obstacle that they could easily drag away, but they stood still.

They stand still because they were tied to a similar chair when they were too small to move it. They remember the failure to move the chair and they believe that they are tethered to a fixed object and that there is no use in trying to pull against it.

We can be affected in the same way. We set up ceilings and walls around us. We limit ourselves and follow the path of least resistance. We allow ourselves to be pigeonholed and we stay tied to the chair. To be a late bloomer, we need to act. We need to pull and untie ourselves from the chair, so we can knock down the walls and break through the ceiling to achieve our goals.

As we get older and have other responsibilities, we tend to be homebodies and not get out as much as we did, socially and for work. We tie ourselves to the chair of social/networking isolation under the guise of being too busy or helping our families. Are we really too busy or helping our families by coming home and flopping in our favorite chair in front of the TV? You should measure how much time you spend in front of the TV. My guess is that you will be shocked. What better things can you do by turning the TV off and doing other things. The flood of information and entertainment that we have today overwhelms us, and we forget that we are social creatures and we thrive around other people.

We also tend to mirror the actions and attributes of the people around us, so it is important to socialize with people with character and varied backgrounds. The adage that it is hard to fly like an eagle when you are surrounded by turkeys is true. If you can surround yourself with people who want to succeed, you will be better off. The challenge that comes with a lack of belief in late bloomers is that you will get a lot of resistance from people in your efforts to improve yourself. Even those who care about you.

Most people are stuck in mediocrity. Very few people will want to do the work that will turn them into a late bloomer. As you are looking for likeminded people, you may even inspire some of your friends and family to join you on the path to becoming a late bloomer. Unfortunately, you will probably find this to be the exception rather than the rule.

From the general crowd, you will hear that you are too old to start a business or that you are too fat to run 5K race or that 40-year-old middle managers can't make it to CEO. The funny thing is that you will hear this most often from the people who care about you. As we discussed before, these people don't want to see you get hurt, so they discourage you from taking risks. Their intentions are good, but their impact is not. If you have loved ones that want to protect you more than support you, you will need to find a more robust support system.

I have suffered this "help." I have had loved ones and friends unintentionally discourage me or make me feel like I've missed the boat. They have done it to try to help me, but it just made me feel insecure and nervous. I have been told by a mentor that I was born in the wrong era. He told me that if I started my career in the 50s, I would have been more successful. Another told me that I was getting a little old to be moving forward. This friend explained how he sold his first company in his 30s. I have been told many times to take the safe way that I have to think about my family.

You can also be your own worst enemy. Even if you were motivated and active when you were younger, you might have become discouraged and tired. You see people who have gotten ahead, and you see where you are, but you have forgotten how far you have come.

We all tend to measure our progress against the progress of others. We can recall from the times when we were kids that sports and games lead to winners and losers in life, success is not so clear. We all have different skills, desires, willingness to work and other factors. A person living in a studio apartment or a person living in a mansion can be either successes or failures depending on other factors in their lives. Our oversimplified perception of success combined with the mixed messages from friends and family can sabotage our success.

I combated this and found success using the techniques in this book. I, like all of you, have had obstacles. I learned by experience that overcoming obstacles can be fun and making sure to listen to the right people make the journey easier and more satisfying.

You will not be able to take away the concern and bad advice from family members and some friends. They care about you, but they do not understand your journey. You don't necessarily want to separate yourself from your family. You need to be careful about what you share and when. This way, you will get to share their company but avoid feeling the criticism.

It is helpful to have a group around you for support and to act as a sounding board. This group does not need a formal support group. This group can be a bunch of friends or networking groups. Success-oriented people are all around you, and you need to find them. Even though it can be informal, it is not optional. You have and will continue to act like the people around you, so you need to surround yourself with people you want to emulate.

Not all of the people who discourage you are doing it with your best interests at heart. Some people will try to hold you back to make themselves feel better. You are not the only one feeling tired and lost. There is a whole group of people that feel that way. They are the gigantic mass of people in the middle who have gotten somewhere but not necessarily to the place they wanted to go. They have moved past the beginning, but they have not reached the destination they expected. They are stuck in the middle. They work hard, but they don't have a plan, they want to succeed but don't want to put in the work. They have experienced setbacks and let those setbacks discourage them. They believe they are destined to be stuck in the middle and don't like the idea of people breaking free of the middle. You don't want to be influenced by their behaviors or take the advice that keeps you stuck in the middle with them, not failures but also not successes.

"A successful man is one who can lay a firm foundation with the bricks others have thrown at him." David Brinkley

When you start to push yourself to achieve your goals, some of the people around you will ridicule your efforts to break free from the mass in the middle and reaching your potential. These people perpetuate the myth that if you do not succeed by a certain age, you are out of opportunities. This mass of people causes inertia that holds others back. They can pull on you like deep mud pulling on your feet as you are walking through a swamp. They do not want you to succeed; they want you to be stuck with them in shared mediocrity. If you succeed, it shows that success is achievable and the people around you have not done it. They would rather believe that success is not possible.

You need to ignore these people, and when possible, you should avoid them. There are enough obstacles to reaching hard goals. You don't need to add additional barriers and traps by associating with people who want you to stay in the middle or worse people who want to see you fail. You need to insulate yourself from people who will hold you back or push you down. You will need to make an effort to find people who want to succeed. Most people are in the gigantic middle and don't believe that people can succeed after a certain age.

It is decision time. Do you want to be a late bloomer or stay on the path of least resistance? Becoming a late bloomer starts with a decision to succeed. Now the work begins. You have to alter your environment to be more open to your success. You have chosen the people with whom you want to associate. You need to focus on you. If you do not work on yourself, you will not get to the places you want to go. Lastly, you need to prepare yourself for success, intellectually and physically. A big part of preparing yourself physically is controlling your diet.

When we have bad diets and are in high-stress situations, we can find ourselves getting sick. Whether it is recurrent sinus infections or irritable bowel syndrome, we can find ourselves out of commission. When I was younger, I suffered from some of these ailments. It is hard to succeed if you are in the bathroom during important meetings or if you are out sick when important decisions are being made. Eighty percent of success is showing up, and if you aren't there you will miss out on opportunities

A major example of this situation in my life occurred almost 20 years ago. I was very sick on the day of an important meeting where I had an important role to play. I decided to call in sick. My absence left the president of the company in a bad place. My calling in sick had a very negative impact on my future with that company. Before the meeting I missed, I was given important assignments on key projects. After I called in sick that day, I found my assignments were not as important and were on ancillary projects. I was sidelined, and my career stalled. If I could do it over again, I would have medicated myself, gone in that day and taken the next day off.

Since we cannot go back in time, I persevered. I left that company and got a fresh start. I learned from that experience, and I now know that when I have responsibility for a task, I need to see that it gets done. I don't necessarily need to do it myself, but I make sure it gets done. That mistake set me back a couple of years in my career. I needed to build it back up. I was still a hard worker, I still brought in results, but that one sick day defines how people important in the company saw me for years to come. It is not just about hard work, it is about the proper image, and many of us don't have the experience when we are younger, and we stumble along. Some are lucky or have training so that they can avoid the pitfalls. The rest of us have setbacks that keep us from getting to where we want to go. By continuing to perform well and persevering, I was able to find success and overcome the obstacles. It would have been easier to be bitter and blame others, but by keeping positive and taking action, I was able to succeed.

Looking back, I have taken risks, and some did not pay off. Some of them put me in financial straits. I was not able to bring my family on vacations or live in a large house, but we did okay. I put in long hours even now, but I found ways to spend time with my family. I have balanced my life, so I have been generally successful even when I have had career setbacks. The key is to keep pushing, getting the right information and moving forward.

I wrote this book not just for you the reader, but also for me. The path of the late bloomer is not an easy one, and we all need reminders to keep us on track. While this book will help you prepare yourself to get to the next step, it is helping me stay on track. Success is a journey as well as a destination. The rest of this book will give you ideas on how to set yourself up for success no matter where you find yourself at this point in your life. Being a late bloomer is not an easy path, and it will be harder for some than it is for others, but it can be very satisfying.

Chapter 2 – Does Success Have an Expiration Date?

You are never too old to set another goal or to dream a new dream.

C.S. Lewis

People are capable, at any time in their lives, of doing what they dream of.

Paulo Coelho

As we discussed in the first chapter, we can be our own worst enemies. We have self-doubt and fears of failure that can keep us from taking the risks we need to take to be successful. This doubt and fear are magnified as we get older and build our own unique set of experiences. These experiences can cause inertia that continues to push us along a particular path. This path can lead us to believe that there is an expiration date on success and that our time to succeed has ended. This is not true!

If this is not the path we want, we can and need to work toward changing our path actively. If we don't, the inertia of our experience will push us farther down the wrong path and away from our goals. It is easy to succumb to this inertia and stay on the wrong path since we have become comfortable with it. We also surround ourselves with like-minded people, so we have constant reinforcement of the false belief that we have to stay on our path even if it means abandoning our true goals.

I think that my experience is typical for many in my generation. The popular culture of the late 1970s to the 1990s had many references to succeeding early in life. We ended up using movie and book characters as the models for the paths we want to follow. It showed young executives as energetic and older executives as stoic and out of step.

We were raised in the eighties when success was being showcased left and right. There were movies about successful people, TV shows about rich people, and we all wanted to be there. I remember an article in Fortune Magazine that addressed young professional's concerns about living on "only" $200,000 a year. This portrait of success is what we were weaned on. There was an expectation of success.

I had all these ideas in my head. I studied business, and I planned my career. I had a lot of interviews at banks, and I thought I was ready to shine. Then there was the S&L crisis. Many, many banks went out of business, and there was a glut of real estate that flooded the market. Professional jobs were lost, never to return, and professionals had to scramble to find their places in other industries. Then there was the outflow of jobs overseas. This reduced many jobs in manufacturing. This reduction in job opportunities had an impact on the career tracks of both blue and white-collar workers.

Many people were left reeling. It was as if they had their ropes cut, and they were left to drift. If they did not start their engines, they were pushed along with the tide instead of getting on a course that leads to their goals My experience immediately after college forced me to make dramatic changes to my plans, but those changed plans led to satisfying jobs and interesting people.

Young, aggressive but naïve people were presented as examples of success that people of my generation wanted to follow. Movies like Wall Street and books like Liar's Poker were supposed to be cautionary tales, but we turned them into anthems for the generation. Earning money at any cost was presented to us as the definition of success. The lessons being taught by the older more experienced people in the movies and books were ignored. It was more stylish to follow the young Turks and ignore the lessons of the experienced people. This message was reflected in the courses we took in college and the careers we chose. We ended up measuring ourselves against movie and book characters. Then we started measuring ourselves against the people we knew.

We saw people who did better than us, and we saw people who don't make it as far, and we gauged our success by that. We did better than Joe, but Ann is doing better than us. We had people telling us that they are proud that we made it this far, but we have that feeling that we did not make it quite far enough. I see this pattern a lot in generation-X men. Our heads were focused on a success that most of us could not reach following the paths we were on. We were dispirited and confused. Many of us gave up on the goals we had and settled into a routine. We had the mistaken belief that we would find that perfect company and would work there for our career, making steady steps up our career ladders.

The environment of regular career advancement changed with advances in technology. Technology increased productivity which reduced the need for additional workers which reduced the need for supervisors. All of these factors reduced the number of paths for generation Xers to get the experience they need to advance when they were younger. When there were a lot of leadership opportunities for people in their 20's, now these opportunities go to people in their 30s.

The structure of the organizations we worked for has changed dramatically over the last 30 years. Organizations are much flatter, there are fewer opportunities for career growth, and there is also less stability. Technology has made the workplace much more volatile. With ISP phones and inexpensive internet connections, offices can be anywhere. These changes have made the workforce more mobile. There are opportunities to work in isolation, and a manager can oversee a very large spread out teams. Flattening organizations have reduced the demand for and in turn the opportunity for managers. This structural change has eliminated the traditional path to career success that we were "promised" by popular culture. We found ourselves working harder for fewer opportunities.

Having to work harder has also had a negative effect on our work/life balance. We are not home at 5:30 for dinner, and we don't have time to do many of the things we want to do. If we want to be able to fund our non-work goals, we need to work harder and longer. If we make time for our non-work goals, we can have trouble affording it. An example is a stay at home parent. It is very hard to afford to raise children without outsourcing part of their care. If your goal is to have a parent stay home, you will need to give up other goals, and you will put a lot of stress on the working parent. It can be worth the sacrifice (my wife and I did it), but there are costs. Having one income makes it difficult to take risks and get ahead. You never want to be caught with no income when you have a family to support, so you avoid taking risks, and your goal achievement can stagnate. This stagnation can lead to giving up on your goals. The choice to push through the anxiety of lost income and the guilt of missing family events can be a hard choice to make. We can easily rationalize our giving up on our goals. There are real, valid reasons to do so. Because of these reasons, it is important that you confirm, you are working towards the goals you want, not just taking the path of least resistance.

We are tired, frustrated and we feel guilty about making choices to do one thing and sacrifice another, and then we see the new articles are now about how we need to promote Millennials. The speed of technology and the changing work environment are the reasons primarily given for why Millennials need to be pushed to the front of the line. The unstated message is that older people need to stand aside and give up on our goals. This message is the next generation of the myth of only the young can be successful. This message is a signal that it is too late for Gen X and Y. This message is not true.

The opportunities are still there. Just as the myths were perpetuated in the past, they are being perpetuated now: The young executive is praised; the teenage scientist is awarded; the 30 under 30 executives are announced not because they are the norm, but because they are unusual. The 40-year-old executive or the 55-year-old board member is not celebrated because that is the expected age for those positions. The Millennial generation may be more equipped to handle technology, but other experiences can't be learned without going through them. They will have their own challenges.

Most people do not have skyrocketing careers. Careers tend to meander back and forth. The key is to move up as you meander back and forth. It is like hiking up a mountain road.

Most people can't race straight up the mountain. To let people hike up the mountain, the trails are cut into the mountain in a meandering back and forth pattern. Meandering takes a lot longer to get to the top of the mountain, and it takes persistence. Many people stop at viewing areas along the mountain to see the sights. They don't carry on to the top. Only the most persistent hikers get to the top and the best views.

The same happens in peoples' careers. They start hiking up the career mountain, and they stop at less than ideal jobs. Some make it just beyond the start and stop, feeling good about where they are. Others struggle to make it farther up the mountain. They see other people being helicoptered to the peak and they get discouraged and stop. It is the late bloomer that keeps driving and pushing. They make it to the top with no bitterness toward the people who got there first. They do not give up, they push forward and reach their goals.

Careers have become the main measure of success. We need to keep in mind that it is not the "THE" measure of success. You may define success differently. Your work-life may be an obstacle to your success. You may be stuck working when you want to be a better parent or a volunteer or do other things. The problem is that unless we win a huge lottery jackpot, we need to work to fund our lives. We cannot donate money if we can't feed our families. One of the quotes from my college experience that has stuck with me came from my business ethics teacher. He said: "The business of business is to do business." What he meant was that a business needs to earn a profit before it can care for its employees and communities. This concept is also applicable to individuals. If we can't afford to bring our family on vacation, we don't get to have the experience of bringing our family on vacation. We need to make choices. How badly do I want to bring my family on vacation? Do I work overtime or get a second job and miss our kids' ballgame? Do I save for a house or do we stay in the apartment? These decisions and the realization that life takes money to live is daunting. We want to follow our passions, but we need to be able to fund our lives. We need to make difficult choices.

As people move ahead, if we don't move ahead at a pace we are happy with, we can get discouraged and feel tired. This discouragement leads to a lack of energy that can keep us from reaching our goals and can be exacerbated by a workplace that does not fit our personality. We can get into a cycle. We get tired which makes work frustrating which tires us more. It can put us into a rut.

If you have ever had your car slide into a rut in the road, you know that it can be a challenge to get your car out. If you have not taken care of your car and you have bald tires and your car doesn't have the power it did when it was new, it can be even harder to get out of a rut. You might even need a tow truck to get out. A rut captures the tire and makes the tire go in a direction you may not want to go, or it keeps you stuck in one spot. It can take a lot of effort to get out.

You can personally get stuck in a similar way. If you have been in the frustration energy drain cycle for a long time, you may not have the energy to get out of the rut yourself. You will need the support of others. You can have a mentor, but if you don't have one already and you are in a rut, it might be hard to attract one. If people are going to mentor someone, they want someone with some energy and who will put some effort into the relationship. To get you out of a deep rut you may need more than a push; you may need a tow. In this case, the tow would come from a career/executive coach.

The coach can give you techniques to get out of your career rut and get you on track to reaching your goals. They are also a good sounding board. When you get frustrated, you can talk to them. By telling someone about your issues, you will feel a burden lifted, you won't be as tired, and you will be able to keep working towards your goals. The coach can also guide you on changing your job to make it more satisfying, or if that doesn't work to help you change companies, so you can be in an environment that will allow you to succeed.

The biggest obstacle for the late bloomer's success can be themselves. By not believing in themselves or by trying to succeed alone, people put themselves at a disadvantage. Success is a team sport. It is very hard to succeed on your own. Having a support system is important. This support system needs to surround you. You need it at work, at home, and with your friends. This does not mean that everyone you experience will be in your support system. Most people will be neutral, and a few will be hostile. You need to cultivate a few key people in each area to help you along. This is a very important part. The metaphor "it is hard to fly with the eagles when you are surrounded by turkeys" is true.

Ideally, at work, you will be able to cultivate a network of people at different levels. You will have people more senior to you, peers and subordinates in your network. People more senior to you can guide you on your career and speak well of you to their peers. In return, you will help them achieve their goals by doing tasks they don't have time to do. You should identify peers that you can work with to achieve your goals while you help them achieve theirs. Your network of subordinates is the inverse of your network of superiors. You support and showcase your subordinates, and they help you achieve your goals by doing tasks for you. If you are in a hostile, anxious or stale work environment, you will have more trouble succeeding than in a supportive work environment.

Continuing this outside of the work plan is important. You need to choose your friends. If you hang out with negative people, you will have a negative attitude. That does not mean that you get rid of friends. You need to manage how you communicate with and how much time you spend with certain people. As you grow as a person, you may find that there are friends you had because they were easy to hang out with but are hurting you more than helping you. As you grow, you will find new friends that are more aligned with your interests. These people will help you achieve your goals.

Your family is also a potential resource for support but can be a negative pull on you. You also need to manage your communication with them. It is important to communicate when there are changes that would affect your family. You can't just drop a bomb on your family like you are moving them to another state. However, if you are single and your extended family gets nervous about change, it might be best to drop it on them at the last minute. By controlling your communication, you can give people enough information that they can help you achieve your goals and leave out parts that will make them nervous and will cause them to discourage you from moving forward.

"I owe my success to having listened respectfully to the very best advice, and then going away and doing the exact opposite." G. K. Chesterton

You also need to be in control of yourself and your thoughts. It is very hard to succeed when you are depressed and feeling bad about yourself. However, that state of mind can act as a slingshot to success when you get out of your slump. Motivational resources use the analogy of a bow pulling back an arrow. You can't shoot an arrow without pulling back the string on the bow. They say it is the same with people. If people have a setback, that setback can act as a bow and shoot them forward. By depressed, I am not talking about clinical depression. That requires treatment. I am talking about the tired, frustrated and hopeless feeling one can get when things are going badly.

"We become what we think about most of the time, and that's the strangest secret." Earl Nightingale

If you have had a prolonged job search and you are not getting the results you want, it is easy to fall into the trap of the lethargy that comes from feeling bad about your situation. You get tired of looking so hard. You are frustrated by the lack of jobs. You then get a feeling of hopelessness that you will never achieve your goals. When one gets to this point, you have reached the point of decision. Do you give up and stay on the path of least resistance or do you move forward on the seemingly impossible path? You may need to change your strategy or learn new skills. You may need to work harder. When we get to the point of hopelessness, we can feel like we are working harder than we really are. We sometimes need a third party to give us a wake-up call and show us we can and need to work harder to achieve our goals. You may need more motivation until you can build discipline.

In my reading and my experience, there is some truth in setbacks propelling people forward. Just remember that this is not an automatic reaction. If it were, homeless people would be millionaires a couple of years later. It does take a lot of thought and focused action. First, you need to get sick and tired of being sick and tired. You need to hit a point where you act. Second, you need to put a plan in place to get out of your rut. It takes focused action to get out of the rut. Third, you need to execute your plan. Nothing happens unless you take action. Finally, you need to roll with the punches and make changes to your plans to reach your goals. Success is not a straight line. You need to be ready to overcome obstacles as you move forward.

As several boxers have insinuated and Mike Tyson said, "Everyone has a plan until they get punched in the face." Everyone is motivated when they first start. It is exciting; you are making a plan and taking action. It is when you hit your first setback that you have your challenge. Then there is a second setback and again and again... Success is not a straight line. There are ups and downs. These inconsistent results can destroy motivation. That is where discipline needs to take over. Motivation is temporary. Zig Ziglar compared it to bathing and recommended doing it daily.

Discipline helps you through the tough spots. You know what you have to do and when you were excited and motivated, you set a plan and started executing it. You set it into your head that you need to do this to succeed. You built a structure for action. Now that you built it when your motivation wanes, you have a framework to follow. If you have built discipline into your structure, you keep going. As you keep going, you build habits. You can build success habits that will build inertia and push you forward to success. After you have gotten up early for a period of time, you find yourself getting up before the alarm goes off. The more you work out, the more you miss it when you can't. You need to develop productive habits like performing breathing exercises when you are stressed out rather than reaching for a Twinkie.

The path of least resistance is the easiest path to take. Most times that path does not lead to success. It leads to the same thing you are getting now. If you are overweight, the path is unhealthy eating and sitting, not healthy eating and exercise. If you are in a job rut, the path is keeping doing what you are doing, not making a change. If you have bad communication with your spouse, the path is being defensive, not open to understanding. The path is the route your habits have built. Habits, positive or negative drive the direction of your path, toward your goals or away from them.

To make any change is hard. Even when a baby has a dirty diaper, they cry when you change them into a new one. Sitting with a dirty diaper although uncomfortable and bad is easier than going through the diaper change. The same happens when we are adults. Being in a job that holds you back or being in an abusive relationship or being on an unhealthy lifestyle becomes a habit, and like the baby with the diaper change, we resist the change.

The good thing is that once you establish a habit, it is hard to break, so you can you use it to your advantage. Once you build a positive habit, you will find that it is hard to break. You miss it if you don't do it and you feel a draw to do it. Habits can lead to excellence, or they can lead to mediocrity. We usually focus on the bad habits because advertisements bombarded us on how to beat bad habits. Smoking, overeating, sedentary lifestyle, etc. are thrown at us as things we need to change. What is the one thing all of these commercials have in common? They all say that their products will make the change easy, but in truth, it is very difficult. Once you acknowledge this path is hard and develop a plan, act while you are motivated. Push through the ruts until you build these actions into a positive habit.

The critics will come back and say the programs don't work. People gain the weight back, they start smoking again, or they are back sitting in front of the TV. We also need to take into account that motivation ebbs and flows. Nobody can be motivated 100% of the time. Once the motivation is gone, if you have not built the discipline, you will fall back into the bad habits. You need to be motivated, then disciplined, then build the habit. Then you will have a positive habit that you won't want to kick. I can't repeat it enough. Success is not a straight path. It is not even a single path. It is a meandering forest trail with obstacles. You can't always see the end of the path. You don't necessarily even have all the tools you need when you start on the path. It can be scary and grueling, but it can also be rewarding and exciting. You need the discipline to stick with it during the scary and grueling times.

It can be hard to find a model to follow. Success means different things to different people, and success needs to be balanced. Would you consider a rich man who alienated his family and is alone successful? Would you consider someone who worked really hard but did not take care of themselves and ended with health problems successful? Being focused on a goal in isolation of your other life needs can help you achieve that goal but does not necessarily make you successful.

You need to define what success means to you.

- Does it mean you want to own a company?
- Does it mean you want to be a great teacher or a great parent?
- Do you want to be an advocate for the homeless or against animal cruelty?

What is success in your mind? Once you have determined what success means to you, you need to make sure you are targeting a balanced success. You also have to determine if you are willing to pay the price for that success. There are always costs even if they are not monetary costs.

There is a concept in economics called opportunity costs. Opportunity costs are the loss of the potential reward from one course of action when one chooses another course of action. Choosing means that you can't experience your kid's sporting event when you need to go to a client dinner that is vital to your company's success. You need to make a choice. Not all the choices are so black and white. You can't go to an exercise class when you choose to go to the bar with your friends. You can't read a book when you choose to watch television. You can't go to dinner with your spouse when you choose to play softball. There are choices we must make, and we need to make sure they help us reach our goals. The choices listed above were not meant to be judgmental. Going to the bar can help you build relationships. That show on TV may be important. The softball game may be your exercise time. The point is to make sure that you understand that a choice always comes with costs.

You need to have ancillary goals to support your main goal. For me, I want to have a senior management position. To get it I need to have the energy to work the hours needed. To do that I need to have fitness and diet goals. I need to have a happy home. To have that I need to live within my means to avoid financial stress, spend time and talk with my family to make sure I am an engaged participant and I need to be as good of a provider as I can be as I am reaching my goals.

It is hard to own a company if you are living out of your car. It is really hard to be a good teacher if you are concerned about the fight you had with your spouse. It is hard to be an advocate for the homeless if you are concerned about being evicted from your home. It is not impossible to succeed, but it does make it harder.

Just because I need those things doesn't mean that I always get it. I took risks that left me with a lot of financial stress. There were times that I was working so hard that I lost touch with my family. There were times that I forgot my fitness and became very overweight. Success is not a straight line. There are ups and downs. These ancillary success goals need to be on your mind as you are achieving your goals, so you have the foundation upon which to build the rest your success. These ancillary goals should also help build the support system we discussed earlier. Remember that motivation wanes and discipline is hard. A support system will help you when things don't go your way.

You will have failures. If you do not, your goals aren't big enough. You may not achieve all of your goals. By pushing your limits, you open yourself up to fail. Failure is scary to a lot of people. The fear of failure, or of ridicule push people to make small decisions. If you want to open a business and people are telling you how risky it is, you may not go for it. Not because it is too risky but because you are afraid of what people will say if you fail. They only know that the guy on TV said that opening a business is hard.

You have information that the others don't. You know what you are capable of, what you are willing to sacrifice, how hard you are willing to work. When developing your support system, you need to take counsel only from people who have experience and have your interests at heart. You need to have honest, experienced advice. Opening a gas lamp lighting company may not be the best idea. But your idea for an innovative website company may be a great one. You need a coach, not an inexperienced advice giver.

You will be amazed at how many "experts" come out of the woodwork when you start talking about doing something different. In my martial arts experience, I heard a lot of people call other styles watered down or ineffective. These people never trained in the styles. They were just listening to the marketing pitch their kids' teacher used to keep the kids in their school. By listening to these "experts", people missed out on having a good teacher with an effective style.

You need to listen to people who are the most experienced, not the loudest. People want others to listen to them. Many people want to feel important, so they talk beyond their experience to make themselves feel important. You need advice that will help you, not pump up the ego of one of your peers. Choose your counselors wisely. Look for experience over enthusiasm when building your support network.

Every year, around my birthday, I look back on the year to see how I have done. I also look back farther to see how far I have come.

Each time I do this, I find that I have achieved a lot more than I remembered. I discover that any failures I have had (even the big ones) did not end my ability to achieve my goals. I intentionally reflect and get a true perspective on how I performed.

We need to believe in ourselves if we are going to push ourselves harder to achieve more. Believing in ourselves can be harder to do if we are focused on areas where we have been less than successful.

Since you have made it that far, you see yourself as a late bloomer. I want you to reflect on your past performance and write down all you have achieved. When I have done it, I used calendars, notes and sometimes asked other people to figure out all I have achieved. It can be slow at first, but as soon as you start to build momentum, you will see that you have accomplished a lot.

Once you see that you have had successes along the way, let's read on to see how we can build a strong future.

Chapter 3 – Escaping the Mediocrity Trap

We are what we repeatedly do. Excellence, then, is not an act, but a habit.
Will Durant

If you are not willing to risk the usual, you will have to settle for the ordinary.
Jim Rohn

As we get older, we gain experience, and this experience is a two-edged sword. The first edge is the knowledge that will help us move forward. The second edge is the "set in our ways" effect. The second edge can hold us back. The second edge includes:

- The habits we build.
- Prejudices against new things.
- Fear of new technology.
- Discounting the comments of those younger than us.

Experience is good and bad. We need the knowledge that it gives us but when we get set in our ways, we put ourselves on the road to mediocrity. If we keep doing what we are doing, we keep getting what we've been getting. If we want to get ahead, we need to leverage our knowledge and embrace change.

It can be hard to determine what are the experiences that will help guide us forward and which ones will hold us back. It is easier just to keep doing what we are doing and stay on the path of least resistance. The way to temper the harmful side effects of experience is constantly learning new things. We must keep learning, or we stagnate. We get set in our ways, and we become less flexible. Learning includes traditional education, taking classes and seminars. It also includes reading. Reading is the original self-paced courses. Lastly, it includes mentor relationships. Meet with people who are doing what you want to do and learn how they are doing it. You will not only learn new techniques to improve your performance you will learn what to avoid.

Learning from other people's mistakes is a shortcut to success. If you can avoid pitfalls, you will move faster. You can learn about other people's mistakes in several ways. You can see it firsthand. You can see what your boss or coworkers do and what the results are. It may seem like common sense, but if your coworkers are doing something that doesn't work, you should do something else. It can be easy to get caught up and go with the flow or be afraid to rock the boat, but if you want to succeed, you need to do the stuff that works.

You can read about people's experience in books. Both fiction and non-fiction expose you to situations that can happen to you. Non-fiction like biographies and books on your profession or avocation will have examples of people making mistakes. These are real-life situations from which you can learn. We can also learn lessons from fiction. These lessons are more general since they are not real-life examples, but they are useful.

You can also learn from mentors. They have their own experience and the experiences of the other people they have mentored. The good thing about mentors is that you can ask questions. You can't ask a book questions, and in classes, you can't always spend a long time on a specific topic, the teacher needs to move on. Mentors give you the specifics you need to make decisions.

All of these learning methods are important. Not only does taking classes give you the information you need, but it also reminds you of the steps in learning. You need to follow a learning process in classes, and those processes have applications in learning outside of the classroom. Reading is a less expensive way to build background information. I have heard teachers say that it takes about 30 books to get a doctorate degree. If you read a book a month on a particular subject, you can get the equivalent of a doctorate degree every three years. Your education is your responsibility. Your decision makes the difference. If you make education a priority, you will remain open-minded, and you will accept the opportunity costs of studying. You will stay flexible and will be better able to succeed. You will have an advantage over your competitors. You will have the experience of a middle manager but the curiosity and learning potential of a new employee. That combination is powerful. In martial arts, we call that keeping the white belt mentality. If you know there is always something to learn; you can remain as excited as a student on their first day of class.

An important component of success that is often overlooked by many people is a physical condition. Hitting the gym helps you in your career. You should have a fitness routine. Fitness helps in a couple of ways. One if you look fit, you will be treated with more respect. It is not fair, but it is the way it is. People judge with their eyes. We are always warned to not judge a book by its cover, but we do anyway. If you are overweight or even hold yourself in a way that makes you look flabby, people will look upon you as slow and lower energy than someone who is fit. Your appearance puts you at an immediate disadvantage.

By being unfit, you are adding another obstacle to your path, and there are enough obstacles already. You cannot afford to add our own. You need to present yourself in a way that portrays the brand you want to show. If you are overweight and get winded walking up the stairs, people will notice, and that will not help you in branding yourself as the up and coming manager or the active parent or even the most helpful volunteer.

Physical appearance also includes the way you dress. Overweight people have less of a choice in fashion. Many times, the selection is not as flattering as the selections available for fit people. Your appearance can further add prejudice against your personal brand. If you look overweight and frumpy, you look even less than the leader you want to be. This is not just the case for success in business. It is everywhere. If you are trying to get education services for your child and you show up at the school wearing stretched out sweatpants and an oversized polo shirt, people will not take you as seriously as they would if you were in dress shirt and slacks. It is the same if you are buying a car or any large purchase. The person you are buying from will look at you, and that first impression will determine the service you get. Again, it is not fair, but it is reality, and it will hold you back.

I was an oriental rug salesman in college. A man came in who was in shorts and shirt looking like he just finished cleaning up a pile of leaves. He drove up in an old Land Rover and wanted to look at rugs. The other salesman did not want to talk with him because they thought he would be a waste of time. It turned out that he was very wealthy and ended up buying $20K in rugs and that was in the late 1980s.

He could afford to look frumpy because he could afford other options. If we are working to get our shot, we need to be right and tight every time. We cannot afford to miss opportunities because we look lazy or sloppy or not too bright. We need to present ourselves in a way that would be accepted by the people we are trying to sell to and no matter what we are doing, what we are selling. In this case, you are selling you. You are building your brand. If you do not know what that looks like, look at how that person is portrayed on TV or in the movies. What does a great teacher look like, what does a great parent look like, or a businessman or scientist? Remember that there is the actor factor. You do not need to look like Brad Pitt or Jennifer Aniston to be successful, but how do they dress, how do they hold themselves. That is how people expect a successful person to look. How you look, and act builds your personal brand.

You have a personal brand whether you know it or not. Are you the person people always call when they need help moving? Or do people roll their eyes when you are assigned to their project team? People see you in a certain way just as they see the brand of paper towels they buy at the store. Are you worth the extra money or do you push the mess around and fall apart? How the people around you perceive you is your personal brand. Are you someone people are attracted to or repelled from? The brand you portray determines that. If you do not control that personal brand, you will be at the mercy of what other people think. I know a person who has a lot of experience and can add value with their knowledge but is afraid to state a firm opinion which leads him to talk in circles. His talking in circles leads his manager and peers to discount his opinion and not take him seriously. This flaw has put a ceiling above him and since he is getting older and losing energy, he will have trouble succeeding in his position and may even have trouble keeping a job at the level he is at now. That person does not control his personal brand, and his brand screams annoying and mediocre. What does your brand portray?

In building your brand, manage your weight the best you can. I know that it is not easy, but we don't have to be athletic. We just need to be fit enough to have confidence. Dress appropriately and act the part. You sometimes have to fake it before you make it so don't be discouraged. If you are overweight or can't afford appropriate clothes, you can still succeed, it is just harder. Try to take all the advantages you can. If you are allowed to wear shorts and t-shirts in the office does not mean that you should. If you are going to a doctor, who has more credibility, the doctor in shorts and a t-shirt or the doctor in a lab coat?.

The other benefit of fitness is energy. The more fit we are, the more energy and endurance we have. When we carry extra weight, especially when we are older we get tired. It turns into a cycle, we lose fitness, and we change our habits to accommodate our lack of fitness. We started waiting for parking places near the store. We take the elevator or escalator even up one floor. We don't work out. On top of that, we have other responsibilities that make it harder to work out, so we avoid it.

We also fool ourselves on what eating healthy means. We eat too much, and we make high-calorie choices. These foods can stay with us, and their digestion takes even more energy. Have you been exhausted after eating a large unhealthy meal? It is hard to get work done after that. If you add alcohol to the mix, it is even harder.

To avoid mediocrity and succeed at whatever you have chosen to do, you need the energy to get the job done. Plans without action do not achieve goals. If you want something different, you need to do something different. Unfortunately, most of us cannot drop what we are doing for a living to achieve our other goals, so we need to do more to get what we want.

"To be successful, you must accept all challenges that come your way. You can't just accept the ones you like." Mike Gafka

Since this book already suggested that you add a lot more to your schedule, it may seem strange that I am asking you to work out too. Working out may seem like another obstacle rather than a means to succeed. To be successful, we need to get more done, we all have a limited amount of time. You may ask can't we just skip the workout? I suggest that you think of your workout as maintenance for both your mind and body. If you never took the time to change the oil in your car and bought the wrong kind of gas for your car, how long would your car last? You would have car problems, expensive problems very soon. Unlike your car, you can't buy a new body every five years.

If you are going to push your mind and body, you need to maintain your body. To maintain it you need to exercise and to eat properly. Like your car, your body will perform for a short period when you are pushing yourself with a bad diet and lack of fitness, but not long enough. Did you ever have your week "catch up to you"? You work really hard all week, sneak junk food at breaks and then need the weekend to recover? You ran yourself into the ground. You can only do that for so long before you start breaking down.

Military personnel train all the time. They exercise outside of their normal duties. That keeps them sharp and ready to react and go the extra mile. We need to do the same. We need to train our bodies to work and endure. Exercise is getting more important with the ability to retire at 65 becoming less realistic. If you need to be working at 70 to maintain your lifestyle, you better have the energy and health to do it. That energy and health are built when you are younger. If you are

40, 50 or 60, it is not too late to get fit. It may be harder, but it is doable, and it is essential if you want to maintain your lifestyle longer.

You should treat fitness as if it were an investment. Your time is valuable. You need to make the most of your time. We are all given 24 hours a day. How you invest that time determines how successful you will be. The workout can seem frivolous and unimportant and a good thing to cut out. If you look at fitness as an investment goal, you will have a better idea of how important fitness is. You can compare it to your money.

You need money to spend now, money for a rainy day and money for retirement. The same can be said about fitness.

- You need the energy fitness gives you today.
- You need the quicker recovery time fitness brings when you are sick.
- You need the future energy to do what you want to do when you are retired.

This investment is both an investment of time and a series of deliberate actions. You need to allocate some time each day to exercise. Fitness is important to keep you limber now and healthy in the future. You also need to think about your diet deliberately. You need to plan your diet and eat deliberately.

It is easy to fall into the path of grabbing junk food to satisfy cravings rather than eating for nutrition. You can still eat tasty food, but it needs to be healthy and in moderation.

Each time you eat healthily and exercise you are making an investment in your future. You are working hard now, and when you succeed, you will want to keep what you've gotten. If you work hard and meet your goal, you don't want to lose it because you have run out of energy or you have gotten sick. Investing in your health now will help you mitigate the risks of future health issues. The fitness plan needs to be determined by your current health and fitness levels. Don't try to go beyond your level right away. Overindulgence in fitness can be dangerous too. Check with your doctor before you start exercising. Fitness is especially important if you are older. Build your fitness over time. It took you years to get out of shape. You are not going to get fit overnight.

This book may seem to be overloading your schedule with an impossible number of tasks. However, you will find that the busier you get, the more you get done. This might seem obvious, but there is more behind it. When you are busy, you get more efficient with your time. We tend to have the timelines for jobs stretch to the time we have. If you put aside a Saturday to clean the garage, it tends to take all of Saturday. If, however, something comes up where you must do something else in the afternoon, you'll find you can get the same task done in just the morning.

You can use this to your advantage. If you schedule more tasks, you will find you get more done. Once you build a habit, you will never miss the time. This means that if you schedule workout time, you will find that you get your other tasks done without any harm. You have found more time by being busy. Being busy is a key to avoiding mediocrity. You need to exercise your full potential to be successful.

"Rarely have I seen a situation where doing less than the other guy is a good strategy." Jimmy Spithill

We all have different talents and skills. Olympic runners are successful. Does that mean we are not successful runners if we do not run that fast? No, we must measure our own goals. If we are capable of and have the goal of running a 5-k road race in under 30 minutes and we do not train, and we miss our goal we are not successful. On the other hand, if we don't train and we do hit the goal, the goal is too low, so we are not meeting our full potential.

You can hit goals and still be stuck in mediocrity. If your goal is to be less than 15 minutes late for work every day and you are only 5 minutes late, you have hit your goal, but it does not help you escape mediocrity. You need to have challenging, meaningful goals that move you in the direction you want to go. Once you have those goals set, you are on your way to escaping mediocrity.

Setting big goals can be scary. We can see failure around every corner and want to stay safe. We put up walls in our minds: no time, wrong skills, obligations, etc., so we don't think we can achieve big goals. We create many obstacles, including limited time, in our minds. If we think something will take a lot of time and we obsess, we will find we spend more time thinking about it and not getting other things done.

If we schedule our time around the things we want to get done, we can get them done. It is a lot like the experiment on whether or not a jar is filled. In this experiment, a teacher fills a jar with rocks and ask the students if the jar is filled. They say yes. The teacher then pours gravel into the jar around the rocks and asks if it is full. When the students say yes, the teacher pours sand around the gravel, and the students are a little less sure that it is full. Finally, to complete the example, the teacher pour water over the sand. That fills the jar. Like that jar, our day has a lot more space than we think.

The way we fill our days has similarities with the jar in the order of which we put things in it. If we fill the jar with sand first (the least important tasks), we will not be able to fit all the rocks in. The same goes for our days. If we fill our days with the little tasks, we will not have room for the big tasks. If we spend our Saturday morning posting memes on Facebook, we won't have time to clean the garage. But if we clean the garage first, we'll find that we have time to go on Facebook before we head out in the afternoon. Prioritize your day, and you will find you get a lot more done without sacrificing your other tasks. You can also use automation and delegation to make the most of your time. If you clean the garage, you have only cleaned the garage. If you first put clothes in the washer, dishes in the dishwasher and tell your kid to mow the lawn and then clean the garage, you will have clean clothes, clean dishes, and a mowed lawn as well as a clean garage.

If you leverage your resources, you can get more done. There is value in delegation, and you can get more done and as you can see in the example above. Delegation does not have to be to a person. You can use technology to enhance your productivity. When you prioritize your day, think of which things are prime for outsourcing or delegation. To maximize my time, I delegate to people and use technology to enhance my productivity. I also outsource. I send my dress shirts out to be cleaned and ironed. Delegation leaves me more time to work on tasks that are the highest and best use of my time and to achieve my goals.

Napoleon Hill wrote, "whatever the mind can conceive and believe, it can achieve." He meant it to show that you can achieve anything you can think of and really believe in. The problem is thought works both ways. If you believe that you are out of shape or all washed up, you are and will continue to be. It is easy to believe that you will continue to fail if you have failed before. It is much harder to believe that you will succeed when you have failed time after time. Self-doubt is a big part of the mediocrity trap. The more you get stuck in it, the more comfortable it becomes, and the more you will want to stay in it. Go back to your reflection on your successes if you need help remembering that you have been successful.

If you do not work hard to control your thoughts when you are trying to conquer the mediocrity trap, you will fall back on the path of least resistance which is to stay in the trap. It can be even harder if you have had easy victories when you are younger and were not as successful later in life. We see this with people who tell the same stories over and over about a job they had or about what a great athlete they were, and if they had only done this or that, they wouldn't be where they are now. They have no plan to move forward. They convinced themselves that they missed their chance. These people are stuck in the mediocrity trap, and they don't see a way out, so they wallow in the "good ole days."

A real-life example involves people of my generation who, like me, were in the mortgage industry before the financial crisis. Many of them were successful, but it was more of a global success than an individual success. All ships rise with the high tide. It is when the tide goes out is when you see who makes it. As the mortgage industry contracted, changed and became less lucrative, people were scrambling to keep the level of success they had before the decline. They held on to a path that was no longer there. Many of those people landed in jobs that they did not like. They suffered from long-term unemployment and were frustrated. The path they were following disappeared, and they were lost in the woods. They were left unprepared and adrift because they did not have a plan. They just rode the wave hoping it would last forever. When it crashed, they had no place to go.

When that happens, you need to change to a new path. You need to make a conscious decision. You can't wait for the path to come back and you shouldn't let other people drag you down their paths. You need to find your new path. That may not be an instant thing. If you are entrenched in an industry that no longer sustains jobs, you need to find something else. You may need to walk back down the path you came from, hop from path to path for a while or blaze your own trail through the woods. You may not experience a catastrophic meltdown of your industry, but there will be economic disruptions that affect you.

You will experience a crisis sometime in your life. You will be pigeonholed at your job, or you will be laid off or fired, or your whole industry can change or disappear. You need to be pragmatic and be ready and willing to change when the time comes. You cannot control your job, but you can control your career. This crisis can appear in many forms and at different levels of severity. Examples include:

- If you are a teacher and a disruptive student is added to your class.
- If you are an expecting parent and you are prepared for one child and you get twins.
- If you were planning to hike the Smoky Mountains and there is a forest fire.

Some things happen that are outside of your control. You need to adapt if you are going to achieve your goals.

Another piece of the mediocrity trap is a lack of focus. What are you trying to achieve and are you actually working to achieve it? Lying to ourselves about our level of effort is easy. Are you working when you are at work? What value are you adding? Are you investing in your career and adding value to your company? Many people start going through the motions and just doing what they think their job is which is usually just the minimum requirements. Many experienced people retire before they leave work. They have a shorter schedule and are looking forward to the times that they are not working. They leave tasks undone and add less value than a less experienced and cheaper employee. Having this attitude will hold you back, and you will not be able to achieve your goals.

That lack of focus and persistence can be the main obstacle to becoming a late bloomer. You keep doing what you are doing, and you reach a point where you are at the top of the pay scale for your job, and you start to feel insecure. You start to see that your company can hire people to do your job for a fraction of what they pay you and the new people may even be able to do it better. These new people have a better handle on new technology, they have more energy, and they bring a fresh look to the job. You are tired, bored, becoming less effective and possibly a little bitter. You are becoming less qualified for your position than the new people.

If you participate in this in-work retirement and become disengaged from your job, you will suffer mediocrity and will probably eventually be fired or laid off from your job. None of us are entitled to a job. We are trading services for money. If we do not provide the necessary service or if we charge twice what someone else does, we are vulnerable to being replaced. It goes back to branding. If you are the equivalent of expensive but weak, soggy paper towels, the new, cheaper and better cleaning paper towels will be bought, and you will be left on the shelf.

Success does not need to mean promotion. You can hold one job over a career and be successful. Many teachers do just that. If you keep up with technology and news and trends in your industry, you can continue to add value and be successful. You can be a goldmine to your company and repository of information, keeping you in demand.

It is the cycle of disengagement that constitutes retiring at work. If you have the entitlement mentality and you do not invest in yourself, you will become less valuable to your company over time as you get more expensive to keep around. As you become less valuable, you will not have access to opportunities, and as you become more expensive, you will be more vulnerable to lay-off. This lack of access will make it very hard for you to achieve your goals and can foster a sense of bitterness. You become bitter because you are not getting what you want. This bitterness leads to you becoming more disengaged from your job. This disengagement can spiral to the point where you may even be hostile towards your company. Disengagement will lead you to become fully entrenched in the mediocrity trap.

The key to breaking this cycle is to know that you have control over it. The point may come where you are so bitter that the only remedy is for you to find a new employer. If that is the case, you should do it. If you feel that strongly negative about your employer, there is a good chance that your employer feels that strongly about you. If that is the case, the situation is usually not recoverable. It would be easier and healthier to get a fresh start. If you take control, you can leave on your terms rather than being laid-off and left scrambling.

This disengagement does not just happen at work. You can get disengaged from family and relationships as well. That leads to bitterness and further disengagement. You need to invest in your family and relationships too.

If you are not <u>engaged</u>, you cannot succeed.

We all go through spells of disengagement. In all areas of our lives. It can hit at any time in situations like these:

Career: We have a bad time at work, and we cannot wait for Friday to come.

Family: The kids do not do their chores, and you have to rush because people are coming over.

Volunteer Work: You are bringing Thanksgiving baskets to the unfortunate in your community, and you are assigned to bring a basket to a family that seems better off than you: a house that is bigger than yours, two expensive cars and a huge TV (true story).

Any of these things can lead to disengagement. The key is to re-engage quickly. Do something that gets your juices flowing again.

It can be something as simple as relaxing over the weekend and being ready to take on new challenges the next week. Addressing the kid's mistakes, get them back on track then enjoy their company and invest your time in them. Be open-minded, the people with the big house may have lost all sources of income and are on their way to being destitute or remember the family in the back-alley apartment when the little girl asked her mother if this means they can have

Thanksgiving after all (also a true story). There are a lot of reasons to stay engaged; you just need to find them.

Eighty percent of success is showing up. Showing up means more than just being there. It is being engaged. You have control over your career even if other people have control of your job. The control you have includes the control over your attitude. One of my mentors told me a story. He said that there was a guy who was late to work and stuck in traffic. He was cut off by another driver and spilled coffee all over his car. He was furious, and he kept his anger all day. He couldn't focus during the day and told his story of negativity to everyone he met. What did this get him? He got an unproductive day, and he did not accomplish his goals, and he made himself look like a negative person to his coworkers. What happened to the other driver? Nothing. The other driver does not even know our hero exists. He went through his day without a care. Our hero lets someone who did not know he even exists rule his day.

Whose fault was it, our hero or the offender? It was our hero's fault. If he just took a deep breath and relaxed, he would not have had an unproductive day, and he could have laughed about the event at the water cooler rather than complain about it. His coworkers would have laughed with him rather than commiserating with or being annoyed by him. You control your attitude and having a good attitude will make it easier to succeed in whatever you want to do.

Having to worry about this mediocrity trap is a relatively new phenomenon. Before the technology spike that improved the ability to measure productivity, people were able to basically hide for their entire career. Come in late, do the minimum, go home on time, get their annual raise and keep going. None of us can afford to do this anymore. Technological innovation has changed all of that. We need to work harder to succeed, and we don't have the luxury of staying in the mediocrity trap and expecting no consequences.

Chapter 4 – Breaking Free and Moving Forward

Success usually comes to those who are too busy to be looking for it.
Henry David Thoreau

I find that the harder I work, the more luck I seem to have.
Thomas Jefferson

Three keys to breaking free of the mediocrity and getting to your goals involve doing more with what you have now:

1. You need to add more value than you are adding now and have that value targeted towards your goals.

2. You need more energy to go beyond what you are doing now. If you are always tired, you will have trouble getting to where you want to be. You need to get yourself in the condition you need to be in to achieve your goals.

3. You need to have the correct attitude, the correct diet, the correct fitness and the correct environment to build the energy you need to get the things done that you want to get done.

We are all service providers, no matter your profession. You need to add value to the process, or you will be less effective at best and expendable at worst. What are you doing to improve the service you provide? If you want to stand out, you need to perform at a higher level. To do this, you will need to know what that organizational value is. How you stand out will differ depending on what you are trying to accomplish.

Remember you are delivering value for the ultimate purpose of benefitting you. If no one knows you completed a task, then you did not deliver the product to your customer. We are looking for a return on our investment. Anonymous work delivers value but other than personal satisfaction, it is hard to benefit from it. Anonymous acts work for donations and works of good will. It does not work in career development. Just working does not set you apart. Mediocre people work too. You cannot have career development in a vacuum. People need to know that you are effectively accomplishing goals before they will help you progress down your path. You need to treat your efforts as a product and the people around you as your customers. You have to provide the product they need (not always want).

- Delivering discipline to your children is a product that the kids need but don't necessarily want

- The report you need to complete for your boss is something he wants but going the extra mile on it shows something he didn't even know he needed.

- Presenting classwork in a way that keeps students engaged is something they needed but did not even know they wanted.

The value you produce must be delivered. It is not always something that is wanted, but it is needed. You can add the most value by delivering things that people did not even know they needed or wanted. People will have a vague understanding of what they want/need. If you can translate that want/need into a specific reality, you have added a lot of value and have shown that you are someone worthy of notice.

What you need to do in order to add value will be dependent on your goals. If you want to be a better parent, you may have the goal to spend more one-on-one time with your kids. You work hard to give your kids what they need to live. What are you willing to do beyond that to get to the next level? You may need to stop doing things you are good at if they are not getting you closer to your goals. I happen to be good at translating business needs into system designs. The problem is that I do not like doing it and I don't want that path. I found myself getting pigeonholed into that kind of work and that was hurting my chances to achieve the goals I wanted to pursue.

To get out of that trap, I started to focus on the base skills when talking to people.

- I have led interdepartmental, multiple discipline projects
- I have strong analytical skills
- I have strong communication and writing skills

By focusing on the base skills, I was able to get out of the systems side of things and get more into the people side of things which is where I wanted to go.

You need to determine what you want to accomplish and find the keys to achieving those goals.

You need to think about the base skills and how you can apply them in unconventional ways to set you apart and help you succeed where others fail.

- You are a teacher, and you have reached the kids. You may need to reach out to the parents to get them involved to get to the next level.
- You are a manager. You want to get to the next level. Take on projects outside of your normal duties to show you have what it takes.

You'll notice that these value-add projects are visible in the way you want them to be visible. You are building a brand. You are exploiting your experiences and are enhancing them by gaining new knowledge and experience. Taking a class adds to your knowledge, but until you use this knowledge and it becomes visible, it adds no value to you. It does not help you to deliver your product to your consumers whether those consumers are your boss, your kids, your spouse or your friends. Don't go to the extreme and start to think of life as transactional. We don't offer our children love in exchange for something, and we shouldn't start to. Equating our actions as products makes it easier for us to improve them. If we see our love is a product that our family needs, it is easier for us to look at it objectively and improve it. For example, if we can see that being more attentive to our families when we are home increases the quality of their lives, we can make changes that improve their lives without too much of a cost to our own lives.

Delivering this extra value does have costs. Even being more engaged at home costs you the opportunity to decompress and do nothing for a while. It takes energy to do extra work. We can't expect to complete tasks if we don't have the energy. We need to take care of ourselves if we expect to be able to take care of others. You can't be engaged with your family if you are too tired to even get out of bed. You can't drive your car forever without stopping for gas, and you can't expect to get more done if you do not increase your energy. You need to do more so you need strategies to increase your energy.

To boost and maintain energy, you need the proper fuel. If you feed your body junk food, you will not have the energy to keep going. Unhealthy food puts a drag on energy. You may get an early boost from it, but you feel tired and heavy later. That heavy feeling can keep you from going on a walk with your family or going for a workout. It can also cloud your mind, making your mind sluggish and slower to respond to stimuli. By having a poor diet, you are sabotaging your energy and in turn, sabotaging your ability to succeed. If you know any people with diabetes, you can see how an imbalance of sugar can change them. This happens to a lesser degree to people with healthier sugar levels. Diet has a direct effect on how one feels and how they react to situations. Bad diet choices can have a negative effect on attitude and can have a negative effect on how well you work and sleep, which can also sabotage your attitude.

Being fit also affects how successful you can be. Working out releases endorphins which can make you feel better and give you needed energy. Being more mobile also helps you feel better. I am inadequate shape but am looking to improve. When I am with my peers, I can do a lot of things that they cannot, and they blame their age. The problem is that they are younger than me. If I can do things that people younger than me can't, it is not age that is keeping them from doing it. It is the level of fitness that keeps them from doing it. Now I am a lot less fit than I was three years ago. Is it because I hit some age threshold and it is all downhill from here? No, it is because I did not make fitness a priority for me over the last three years. It is funny because one of my peers that complained about age has now surpassed me in fitness because he did make fitness a priority. Now he is helping me get motivated to get back on the fitness track.

There is no offseason when you get older. When you were younger, you could do a sport and then take a season off and get back to it the next season. You can't do that when you are older. Life is like canoeing upstream. If you stop paddling, you get swept back downstream. As you get older, the stream gets faster. You need to keep paddling if you are going to keep doing what you want to be doing otherwise you will just get further and further from your goal. If you are not growing, you are dying.

Your environment also has a great deal to do with your energy levels. If negativity surrounds you, you have less of a chance to succeed. If you are surrounded by people who commiserate about being too old to do anything, you will start to feel the same way. When you get into your late forties and early fifties, you find that people you went to high school with are now grandparents and some have died. You may be a grandparent too. If you were like me, you picture grandparents being people in their 60s and 70s, not their forties and fifties. Because of that, we can project our age to that of a 60 and 70-year-old.

Just because someone is a grandparent does not mean that they are old. It is tragic, but people do die young. Just because some of your peers have passed away does not mean you are too old to accomplish goals.

If you surround yourself with people and things that try to convince you that you are too old, you will have trouble overcoming it. No matter what your age, if you are in an environment that is negative, it will drain your energy. It can be tiresome and depressing being in a negative environment. If you are going to succeed, you need to make every effort to get out of that environment.

If you have a negative attitude, thinking that the world is against you, you will have trouble succeeding. You need to have an attitude that you can and will succeed if you do the right things. You may not know what those things are yet, but you will succeed when you find them. Without an attitude that says you can succeed, you will not succeed. Your brain needs to be onboard. When you have the right attitude, and you are enthusiastic, that will build the energy you need.

Have you ever been exhausted, then found you had the opportunity to do something you really wanted to do? You probably felt one or both of the following. First, you get a boost of energy, and you are ready to go for it. Two, you feel even more tired because you want to do something, but you feel you can't because you are too tired. You almost certainly felt the first when you were younger. You came home from a hard day at school, and you just wanted to go to your room. Then it is time to get ice-cream. You are all of a sudden ready to get up and go. You may have felt the latter as you got older. You had a hard week at work, and you had the opportunity to see your favorite sport, how did you react. These reactions are all attitude. You were tired, but you became untired when you got excited (or more tired). You control that whether you know it or not. Your attitude can make or break you.

Your environment can have a dramatic impact on your energy levels. Negative environments can suck you dry. These negative environments can attack us from all angles:

- a toxic workplace,
- a parents' group that ends up whining about how bad their kids are
- a weekly poker game that ends up being a bitch session over how the members missed their chances to get ahead.

Those environments can foster a negative attitude in you and become an energy drain that can keep you from getting done the thing you want to achieve.

The path to achieving your goals is to add value by doing more things. To do that you need the energy and attitude to get you going. Doing things, the way they have always been done it is the kiss of death for the late bloomer. Things change faster now than they ever have in the past.

Technology changes, jobs migrate, productivity increases, industries are born and die. The only constant is change. If you do not move with the change, you will be left behind. It is important to keep an open mind to change, to change when it is appropriate and embrace positive change.

Changing for the sake of change is not the answer either. Following fads will just wear you down and will not get you to where you need to go. It is a challenging balancing act. Having an open mind means that you will thoughtfully embrace change, not throw everything away and start again each time a new fad comes out. You need to leverage your experience and embrace change to find the correct path.

To be open-minded, you also need to be informed. If you don't know what the changes are, you cannot embrace the change. You will find that you will be dragged along, willingly or not by those who are informed of changes. You probably have experienced this if you work for a larger company. All of a sudden there is a new initiative for productivity or morale or respect in the workplace. These changes can seem to come out of nowhere and often do not seem to make sense.

Working hard and keeping your nose to the grindstone can be good but you cannot just work and stick your head in the sand. You need to be versed in the innovations that are hitting your industry. Both in your company and industrywide. You need to know that there are concerns about productivity or respect in the workplace. You also need to know about trends and programs outside your company, so you are not surprised by changes and if asked can contribute to the conversation. You need to think about solutions before you need them. If you can get to the point where you have an idea of what is going to happen and have a set of recommendations, you will have added more value than you do now.

Part of open-mindedness is flexibility. Now flexibility is applicable in both the physical and mental ways. To maintain youthful energy, you need to be flexible in mind and body. Being mobile is just as important as being mentally sharp in maintaining energy.

Things constantly change, so you need to be able to adapt and thrive in an environment of constantly moving targets. You need to be pragmatic and flexible. We can get set in our ways, and if we try to bull our way through life, we will get a lot of resistance and not succeed. Flexibility does not mean to just go with the flow. We need to blaze our own path, but we need to read the signs and adjust our plans to meet our goals.

It is a fine line. We need to stay on our path to reach our goals but as our environments change we need to be flexible in our approach to getting to our goals. We need to roll with the punches. Flexibility does not mean rolling over and playing dead. Flexibility helps get you through the storm. Think of a tree on a hill. That tree has to be able to withstand the winds and stay rooted. You need to do the same. You stick to your goals and your values, you are rooted, but you are able to flex in the winds and withstand the resistance.

In a dynamic environment, you cannot be rigid. The winds will eventually break you. If you find yourself in constant storms, you may need a new environment. If your workplace in a constant tornado, you will eventually lose your roots and will become ungrounded, but typically storms come and go, so you need to be able to weather them. Our workplaces contract as much as they expand. We have to do more with less, and we must adopt new technologies. If we are not flexible, we will break.

The same happens in our personal lives. We have our values and personal goals, but the world is a constant whirlwind. We are buffeted by negative thoughts and ideas that violate our values. We are given choices that do not meet our needs, and our families are exposed to situations from which we want to protect them. We need to stay rooted but remain flexible to succeed. If we allow outside forces to direct us, we will be pulled in directions we don't want to go. It is easy to get dragged along with the crowd. If you keep to your values and you remain flexible, you can withstand the storm, and you can get what you want without changing your values or compromising your goals. Roll with the punches.

We need to remember flexibility is not just a function of the mind. It is also a function of the body. It is hard to be successful if you feel old. A lot of obstacles confronts us, and as we have said, we don't need to give ourselves anymore. We can't always control our physical condition. If someone is in a wheelchair or has another disability, they can still succeed, it is just harder. It is one more obstacle that needs to be gotten over. We need to be flexible enough to play the hand dealt to us. There will be people who have an easier time than we do. It is not fair, but it is reality. We need to be flexible enough to roll with the punches and be determined enough to reach our goals.

If you are healthy but just let your body go to seed, you are giving yourself a self-inflicted obstacle. It is hard to be confident if you have trouble getting out of bed in the morning and your joints have more snap, crackle, and pops than a bowl of Rice Krispies. I was at a conference after a bad flight and a bad night's sleep. I had gained a bit of weight, and my flexibility was not what it should have been. I dropped my notebook in the hotel lobby, and it took a bit of effort to pick it up. The bellman actually came running over to help me.

Thankfully, I picked it up before he got there, so I wasn't too embarrassed by my difficulties picking up my notebook.

It is not strength or speed that makes you feel younger; it is flexibility. Being able to bend over and tie your shoes without having to sit down. Picking up the notebook without an issue are all things that make you feel better about yourself and give you the confidence to do things that you may have considered yourself too old to do in the past. It is believing that you can do something that helps you actually accomplish it. If you need to meet 20 people over three days at a conference, your ability to walk the miles back and forth in the convention center and being able to sit down and stand up with ease, set you apart from your peers.

While others are huffing and puffing, you are out there getting it done. You can set yourself apart from your competition by being in a little better shape and having a bit more energy. Think of life as a horserace. The winner gets a prize twice as large as the runner-up, the runner-up gets a larger prize than the third-place winner. Did the winner work twice as hard as the runner-up and four times as much as the third place? No. Many times, there is a race to the finish. The first, second and third place winners are right on top of each other. Inches make the difference. The winner can be 1 inch ahead of the other two horses to win. It is the smallest of margins that can keep us from having the success we desire. Giving ourselves every advantage we can is important because your success may require you get ahead one more inch than your peers can go.

Our biggest asset, experience, can be the worst enemy of flexibility. As a late bloomer, you have been around a while and have seen things your younger peers have not. Whether you are cognizant of it or not, you have learned things as you have gone through life that will help you succeed. It may be a long list of things not to do, but there are things in there that you should do.

As we have discussed, experience is a two-edged sword. It gives us the information we need to succeed, but it can also put you in a state of mind that makes you less flexible. It is easy to get into the "we have always done it that way" mentality. This is especially true for people who have been successful and rewarded at lower levels of an organization. You are trained to believe that certain actions are the path to success. Those traits are positive for people who stay in the jobs they have, but if you are moving up in the organization, those traits can hold you back.

The easy example is growth in a sales organization. You can be a top-notch salesperson but be an awful sales manager. The skills that make one a great salesperson do not necessarily translate well to sales management. If you want to move up in a sales organization, you need to preserve the skills you learned as a successful salesperson but be flexible enough to learn the skills you need to be a sales manager. Some of the sales skills are transferable, but they are different enough that you need to be flexible.

Your experience as a salesperson gives you credibility to your new subordinates. Your sales skills will allow you to help your team members when they are struggling with a tough customer. You can go in and help close the sale. What are the skills you need to learn?

Coaching. You need to be able to keep your people motivated and effective.

Teaching. You need to be able to share your experience with others to scale your effectiveness.

Measuring. You need to be able to track and measure the effectiveness of your people and to determine if the changes you make are effective.

Leadership. You need to be able to lead your group.

Collaboration. You now have responsibilities beyond sales. How are you going to work with the leaders in other areas of the company?

If you are performing a project around the house, there are certain tools you need. I just installed a dishwasher in my kitchen. I opened the box, took out the instructions and sat down and read them. The instructions told me what tools and parts I would need, so I gathered all those items and organized them accordingly. When I was putting in the dishwasher, I ran into some very frustrating situations. When I got frustrated, I took a step back and a deep breath. That cleared my head, and I was able to get back to work. The same things are needed in your career. You need to take an inventory of your skills and experience when you are starting a new project. If you don't have some of the skills, you need to research and find out how to do what needs to be done. When you hit rough spots, you need to step back, take a deep breath and then get back to work.

What is better than experience? More experience. The more you know or have experience with, the better equipped you will be to get done whatever needs to get done. It takes a lot of time to get experience, but there is a way to get the knowledge experience brings more quickly. It is to learn from the experience of others. It is always to continue to learn new things. There are many ways to do this. You can read technical manuals, read other books from biographies to fiction, take classes, and enter mentor relationships.

Reading technical manuals can get you the work skills you need to get ahead. These can be anything from public speaking books to computer program guides. These books give you the base skills you need. For example, if your job needs you to have Excel skills, it makes sense to get a book on using Excel to quickly get the skills you need to get your job done. There are also soft skills like interacting with others and leadership. There are technical books on those subjects, but there are other ways to learn those skills.

Reading biographies is a good way to do it. I really like Teddy Roosevelt. I have read many books about him, and I emulate some of the traits he exhibited. I saw the leadership and other styles he had, and I learned from it. He also did some things that I find despicable. I don't emulate those traits. You can also learn from fictional characters. Just because a character never existed does not mean that you can't learn from them.

Classes can also be a great resource. The availability of classes today is greatly due to technology. They range from videos on YouTube through more organized videos on sites like Khan Academy (www.khanacademy.org). There are also instructor-led classes online, so you get the benefit of having a teacher you can ask questions. There is also the traditional brick and mortar classroom style classes. These range from for-profit classes like Dale Carnegie or other companies to community provided classes and four-year colleges. There are so many options out there that there is no excuse not to take some kind of classes. Many companies will even pay for the classes.

The last and least used form is the mentor relationship. There is nothing like real-world experience that can be used to help you learn the ropes. A mentor is a person who shares their experience to help you to traverse the maze that is your career. There are pitfalls everywhere. If you can avoid those pitfalls, you can be more successful more quickly. Also, you don't need to be a young person to have a mentor. Your mentor does not even need to be older than you. People get experience at different rates. Do not let your ego get in the way when trying to acquire information. Technology is a good example. You may find someone half your age who can show you how to use technology more effectively. Don't pass up that opportunity just because you feel you are superior to the younger person just because of your experience.

Finding a mentor starts with your network. Consider all the people you know and apply the characteristics you are looking for to the list.

- Do they have the experience you are looking for?
- Do you feel comfortable sharing information with them?
- Are they trustworthy?

Once you identify the person, ask them questions. Start off slow and don't waste their time. Take an interest in them and encourage them to take an interest in you through your questions. Not every relationship will turn into a mentor relationship so you will need to do it over again until you find the right person.

Not everyone will have the time or communication skills to meet your needs. It may be that they don't feel comfortable with you. Don't push a relationship that is not working. Keep the person as a network contact and work with others until you find the mentor that works for you.

Learning is the key to growth and maintaining flexibility. You gain experience faster, and you get the tools you need to succeed in places where you have limited experience. Learning is not easy. It takes time and energy. It is a lot easier to watch TV than it is to take a college course.

How bad do you want it? There is a motivational speaker that talks about the importance of wanting to succeed. To paraphrase one of his stories, a student tells his teacher that he wants to succeed. The teacher brings him to the beach. He tells the student to walk out into the water. When they are up to their necks in the water, the student asks what this has to do with success. The teacher trips the student and holds him under the water for a bit of time. When the student comes to the surface sputtering, the teacher says you need to want to succeed as much as you want to breathe.

The desire to succeed is the first key to success. Desire is what keeps you motivated. If you don't want it enough, you will find a compromise. You will find an excuse to give up. The television will look better than the book on Excel. The couch will look better than the gym. The burger will look better than your weight loss. Your bed will look better than your lesson plans. Without a strong desire, you can't get through the obstacles. The excuses will win.

"You need to want to succeed more than you want to sit on your couch. You need to put it into your mind that you want something. You need to have it in front of you every day." CCB

You need to treat your desire to succeed as a living thing. Desire needs to be fed and nurtured. It needs to grow, or it will die. Think of your desire as a houseplant. You need to give it sunlight, water and feed it once in a while. Otherwise, it will shrivel and die.

- **Sunshine**. You need to see your goal every day. You need to visualize it and have it become part of you. We have all heard out of sight, out of mind. If you are not visualizing your goal every day, it will fade.
- **Water**. You need to nurture your goal. You need to make plans and follow through on those plans. This can also mean micro goals to set a path to your goal.
- **Feeding**. You need to learn more skills to help you turn your desire into reality.

You need to want to succeed more than you want to sit on your couch. You need to put it into your mind that you want something. You need to have it in front of you every day.

You need to feed and nurture your desire, and you need to act on your desire. Action is the next step in achieving your goals. If you do not take action, you will just be a dreamer.

Success takes action. Things are rarely served up on a silver platter. You need to go out and get it. You need to do something to get something. You have determined that you want something. What are you prepared to do to get it? Are you prepared to work for your goal? You need to translate your desire into action.

This can be easier said than done. It is easier and more satisfying in the short term to get what you want now versus getting what you want most. It is easier to satiate the desire to have a donut now than it is the desire to stick to an 18-month plan to get into shape. You have to really want to be in shape to decide against the instant gratification of the donut.

Action also builds momentum. What works in physics works in goal achievement. An object that is in motion tends to stay in motion an object at rest tends to stay at rest. This applies to our goal achievement as much as it does a marble rolling down a slope. The more action you take, the easier it is to continue to take action. We have all heard things like that guy is "on a roll."

Once you get going, it is easier to stay going. Obstacles cause friction. When we run into an obstacle, it is like putting on the brakes or running through mud. We can lose traction and lose our momentum. If we stop and go with our actions, when we hit a pitfall, we are more likely to get stuck. If we are more consistent with our actions, we have a better chance of getting through the pitfall.

Weight loss is a good example of how actions can get you through pitfalls. When we first start our weight loss journey, we are motivated, and we work out and eat right. Then we hit an obstacle. We have to go on a business trip. With a packed schedule, bad sleep in a lumpy hotel bed and big dinners, we go off the tracks with our routine. We fight to get back on the routine then it's Joe's in accounting birthday. Cake for everyone and you don't want to be a stick in the mud. These obstacles keep coming.

Once you have a routine, it is easier. You start working out in the morning, so you get it done before you get distracted by everything that happens in your day. You plan your meals, so you are better able to stay on track. Your eating habits change, so you are not as tempted by the treats at work. You start to see results, and you start feeling rewarded. You are building momentum, and you are better able to overcome pitfalls because you have built momentum.

It is important that you do something. I wanted to write this book. Writing a book takes hours upon hours of work. How can a busy person fit more hours of work into their schedule? I did it by committing to writing at least 10 minutes a day every day. I hit obstacles. When I was at a conference, I was exhausted in the morning, and I sat there for 10 minutes and wrote about 30 words. Not every day will be productive.

Many times 10 minutes turns into 30 minutes or longer. Some days I am on a roll and write 600 words in the time I allow. I have built momentum, and I make a point to get up at 4:45 every morning so I can get done the things I want to get done before my family is awake and before I need to work and will be distracted until it's time to go to bed.

You need to determine what is the best time and ways for you to take action. Nothing gets done until you make the decision to do something.

Chapter 5 – Fitness: Appearance and Performance

Today I will do what others won't, so tomorrow I can do what others can't.
Jerry Rice

Fitness is about so much more than exercise. It is a catalyst for positive change and it affects every aspect of your life.
Amanda Russell

When I was young, I was an insurance agent. I was sent to an insurance company for training, and when I was in training, I had a session that I remember over 20 years later. One of the insurance trainers introduced a successful insurance executive. When he was introducing him, he said this man is a gentleman; he is always wearing a suit. That struck me. Wearing a suit does not make a man a gentleman, but he looks like a gentleman. A person dressed professionally is what people see as a gentleman. There is a man in my church who always wears a suit. He looks like a gentleman. How we present ourselves matters.

It is not just the way we dress. Our level of fitness will determine how people view us. I, like many people, have struggled with my weight. I have been very overweight at various times and relatively fit other times. I have transitioned back and forth so many times that my personal brand reflects that I have always just lost some weight. There are times that I look more energetic than other times. When I do look more energetic, people think that I have lost weight even if I haven't.

As we discussed before, energy is a very important factor in getting ahead. It is not only the fact that you have the energy, but it is also the branding that you have energy. If people think you have energy, they are more likely to offer you more responsibilities and opportunities. You need to have the appearance of having energy. Even though at the time of this writing I am on the less fit side of my ups and downs, I have been able to continue my appearance of having energy because of my involvement in martial arts and my recent competition sparring. This appearance does have an expiration date. If I cannot keep up my level of energy or I stay unfit too long, I will lose my brand of having energy and might compromise my advantage.

We all judge with our eyes. Who looks like they have more energy, an Olympic sprinter or the guy at the picnic with a big gut and no shirt. That does not make the guy at the picnic less competent in his profession, but it does give the Olympic sprinter an advantage with first impressions. Can we succeed if we don't look fit? Yes, we can. Does being unfit constitute a self-inflicted obstacle? Yes, it does. As I have said several times before, we need every advantage we can get. Fitness is generally in our control. If we can, we should overcome that self-inflicted obstacle.

It is hard to get things done when you are sick and tired. Have you ever gone out for a few beers on a Friday night and have to do a cumbersome chore like clean the garage on Saturday morning? Especially if you were out later and drank more than you normally do, you are probably not very motivated to work on Saturday morning. You feel tired, a little heavy and your brain is foggy. Now let's change that work from cleaning your garage to doing your taxes or preparing an important client presentation. How capable are you?

We tend to do this to ourselves every day. It may not be as extreme as drinking all night, but we do sabotage ourselves. We overeat takeout food and stay up late watching Netflix before a client meeting. We don't exercise and end up wearing uncomfortable tight clothing all day. We sabotage our success by adding obstacles and distractions to our everyday life. They are so commonplace we think of them as part of our life, not as things that we can fix.

We are tired around 3:00 every day, and we say it is because we are getting old rather than looking at it and seeing it is because we had a heavy lunch, we doused ourselves with caffeine all morning, and we were up late watching TV and eating pizza. These eating habits sabotage our success. It is hard to be productive when your mind is foggy or if you are feeling sick and tired.

If we analyze it, most of us will find that our fatigue and sickness are self-inflicted. We do not get enough sleep, we eat too much, and we eat the wrong things, and we avoid exercise. These activities destroy our energy, especially as we get older. I was out with some friends. It is OK to go out with friends and drink and eat badly as long as you know the opportunity cost. Your night out will cost you a productive morning. The universal comment was that we could not drink and eat as much as we used to. As we get older, we get more sensitive to changes.

There is no offseason. If you played sports as a kid, you were able to take it easy in the offseason. You would work really hard for the season, and when it was over, you would take a break. As we get older, we can't afford an offseason. We need to be consistent in our quest for fitness. With all the things going on in our lives and our bodies' resistance to change taking an offseason puts you behind and it is very hard to catch up.

We do not have 3 hours a day to train. We have work, family and other commitments. We have a certain amount of time to work out, so we need to be consistent, so we do not lose what we have built. Have you ever worked on a computer document for hours only to realize you forgot to save it when your computer crashed? How did that feel? If you are like me, you are angry at the computer and yourself. Also, if you did not allow yourself enough time to complete the task, you are now behind the eight ball and are under a lot of stress. The same goes for your body.

If you postponed getting in shape and you ate a heavy meal and had a few drinks at dinner the night before a big meeting, and you get to the convention hall only to realize you must walk nearly a half mile to get to your appointment, what happens. From experience, I'll tell you that you arrive at your meeting out of breath and sweaty. If you are meeting someone for the first time, how does that look? At the time, I was lucky. I got there early, so I was able to wash up a bit and catch my breath before the meeting, but I felt sweaty in my suit all day. It was a distraction I could not afford.

It is not just for business. If you are out of shape and there is an emergency like evacuating a stadium or an airport, are you ready to make the march to safety? Would you be able to walk down ten flights of stairs then run a half mile to safety? If not, how are you going to handle an emergency? What if you are a parent or grandparent with little kids in an amusement park? Would you be able to walk the entire length of the park and make it to your car? That is a requirement for a thunderstorm.

Your fitness is important for your success. It is also important for your longevity. My friends and I were joking that we will be able to retire about three years after we die. Many of us will not be able to or will not want to retire at the traditional age. Are you in good enough shape now to believe that you could continue working when you are 70? If not, what are you going to do if you reach 65 and you realize that you don't have enough money to retire? Even if you are a prudent saver, things can happen that would require you to continue working. You may also want to continue working.

As a late bloomer, you may not hit your stride until you are in your late 50s. You may find yourself at 68 loving what you do and not even imagining retirement. Will you have the stamina to continue? Of course, there are health issues that hit us unexpectedly that could curtail our ability to continue, but in general, are you setting yourself up for continued future success or are you setting yourself up for disappointment and failure later in life. Think of today and tomorrow. There are both short and long-term benefits of fitness. Also, you are never too old to start. If you are in your 50s or 60s, it is not too late to get healthy. It may be harder than it would have been in your 30s, but it is still worth the time and effort. You get the same short and long-term benefits.

Expectations are the first step towards or away from an opportunity. If you and other people expect you to succeed, you have more of a chance of succeeding. Underdogs succeed too, but the underdogs believe in themselves and have high expectations of themselves. These expectations are helped or hindered by your level of fitness.

It is hard to expect yourself to succeed if you are sick and tired. If you have trouble getting out of bed, get winded walking up the stairs, or have to unbutton your pants to tie your shoes, you will think of yourself differently than the person who gets up early and goes for a run. The problem with this comparison is that the person who gets up to go for a run probably has different goals than you do. Using myself as an example, I knew a lot of people who would exercise daily, but they had two income households and sometimes had help from family members. I had to commute 40 miles each way in traffic to my job. Could I have gotten a job closer? Not if I wanted to keep the lifestyle I wanted for my family and stay in the industry I have worked in for over 20 years.

To remain fit, I needed much more discipline than the guys I knew who would go running in the morning. I would wave to them as I was driving to work because I needed to leave so much earlier than them. That is when I started to get up at 4:45 every morning. I would do some warm-up exercise and prepare for the day. After I took a productivity class, I added inspirational reading and writing to my morning routine. This was not a perfect solution. At the time of this writing, I have gained a lot of weight from the stress of a job transition, overindulgence over the holidays and the re-establishment of bad eating habits. I am still in better physical condition than many of my peers, but I am not where I want to be. Having been in better shape, I know that I could have more energy and could accomplish more if I were to get back to my ideal physical condition.

As I mentioned earlier, the expectations people have of me have carried over. As a martial arts blogger, I have a couple of videos online, and as a competitive martial artist, some of my peers have posted videos of my fights and forms (kata) competitions. These videos signal to people that I have more energy; that I am competitive, that I want to succeed, that I work hard. That is the message I want to send.

Yes, I want to get fit for me. I want to be healthy, and I want to be able to do more things when I get older, but I also want to send a message. I want the people around me to know that I have the energy, persistence, and determination to help them and through that work, succeed myself. Besides the actual work you do, how you behave outside the job means something too. You want to signal that you are more than the job you are in now. If you are not, then why would anyone move you to something bigger. Again, this is not just about a career. If you are known as an active, informed parent, the teacher will be more responsive in your parent-teacher meetings. If you are able to move around with ease, you can be a more active volunteer. If you can stay on your feet all day, you can be more involved with your kids or as a teacher.

The expectations people have of you also make a difference.

- If you come into your office late every day because you have trouble waking up and getting to the job that sends a message.
- If you are walking with your boss talking and you get out of breath, that sends a message.
- If you get home from work and don't have the energy to play with your kids or to help them with their homework that sends a message.

The longer that you send that message, the more that expectation is set. There have been times in my life that the expectation my kids had was that dad is always tired. I would spend time with my kids, but I would not be 100% there. Work or financial stress would always be in the background, and even though they were little, they had expectations of what I was capable of doing.

Everyone will have expectations of you positive or negative, just like you have expectations of others. To build new expectations takes energy. Unless you can afford to make drastic life changes, you will need to find more time and energy to go above and beyond what you are doing now. To build more energy you need to be fit. Eating properly and getting moderate exercise will provide you the energy to be a better worker, be able to parent more effectively when you get home, take that self-paced excel class after the kids go to bed and to get up early enough to prepare for your day and get to work on time. You do not need to be a marathon runner or a cross-fit champion to have more energy. Eating healthier and working out a few times a week will get you where you need to be.

Chapter 6 – Growing and Expanding Your Horizons

Opportunities don't happen. You create them.
Chris Grosser

Whenever you see a successful person, you only see the public glories, never the private sacrifices to reach them.
Vaibhav Shah

If you are not growing, you are dying. Water that lies undisturbed goes stagnant. Air in a closed space gets musty and a mind that is not learning atrophies. Learning is a skill. It is about adapting to new environments or situations. Like any skill, if you do not practice it, you do not get better at it. You actually start to lose the skill. Starting to learn again is like riding a bike. You can get back on the bike and start riding. That does not mean you start at the level where you left off. If you rode a bike competitively when you were younger, and you stop for 20 years, do you think you will be able to start riding at the same level you stopped?

The same goes for learning. If the last time you took a class was in college 20 years ago, do you think that you will be able to thrive in the new training program your company wants to put you through? If you haven't read a book for information in 20 years or worse, haven't read a book at all, do you think you will be efficient at absorbing information from the book?

Since you are reading this, you do see the value in reading books for learning new things. Reading this book should not be a one-time event. You should be reading all the time. A trainer friend of mine once told me that you need to read about 30 books to get a Ph.D. in a subject, so if you read thirty books on a subject, you have done the equivalent work of a Ph.D. study. That may be a bit of an exaggeration, but there is a material point to it. Reading 30 books on a subject gives you a lot of information on a subject. Since the average person does not read that much, by reading 30 books, you make yourself an expert in the subject as compared to your peers.

Think about what you can learn if you started reading today to expand your knowledge base. If you are rediscovering reading as a learning source shoot for reading one book a month, at the end of the year, you will have read 12 books. If you read a lot now, shoot for two books a month. I happen to read a lot, and I also listen to books on my iPod. By surrounding myself with books, I always keep reading in my mind. I try to read in all formats I can. I have an e-reader, but I also buy books, hardcover, and softcover and as I mentioned audio. Periodicals can also get you information in bite sizes, but they do not dig down deep enough into the story to get you a solid understanding of a subject.

Reading also keeps your mind fresh. You don't need to read stuffy technical tomes that even a proficient reader can only read three pages before getting tired. There are many styles of books and some subjects and styles that might surprise you. The act of reading helps build your skills. Reading for education doubles that experience by helping you practice a skill while learning new information. By doubling down, you are really leveraging your time, and if you can also do it for recreation at the same time, you are tripling your effectiveness. You are training your brain to absorb information, you are learning new things, and you are relaxing.

The subject you are reading does not have to be an exact match on your study topic. A book on politics can help you in your business career. A book on arts and crafts can help you in teaching. A book on manufacturing can teach you about process control. A book on military actions can teach you about strategy. You will also find that expanding your reading base will also open up areas of curiosity that will help you identify what you may want to be doing for your career. Learning is fundamental, and reading can be the first step toward a broader base of learning.

There is a surprising place to learn examples of different situations and people and how to handle them, reading fiction. Fiction gives you the opportunity to see people in different situations and how they act. No matter if the story is on the battlefield, in space, in a romantic restaurant or a workplace, the stories will have people in different situations. You even have books like <u>Animal Farm</u> or <u>Watership Down</u> that use animals, but the characters represent people. The most important part of success is interacting with people so the more you can experience people the better.

I enjoy reading fiction. It helps me relax, and it keeps my mind stimulated. Even though I don't expect to be fighting in an intergalactic battle, I have learned some ideas on how to lead people and have some examples of how people react to stressful situations. These are skills that I need for everyday interactions. For the character, the stress may be the warship engine blowing up. In real life, it can be a person who is having trouble with a career-changing presentation. If you have never comforted someone who had a loved one die, having read about it in a fictional account can give you a baseline to start with. How you talk to your child about a failure to make a sports team or a student on how to bounce back from a failed test performance from characters you have read about.

Fiction gives you access to life experiences that you have not and sometimes cannot have. The more life experiences you have, the better you will be at dealing with situations as they come up. These fictional life experiences can also help with the flexibility we talked about in an earlier chapter. You will be able to see situations from different perspectives. In a pirate book, you can see from the perspective of the deckhand or the captain; the pirate or the pursuing naval captain all in one place. If you are a leader, it is important for you to be able to see the world through the eyes of your employees. If you are a worker or an aspiring leader, it is very important for you to see from the eyes of your leaders. You need to be able to serve your constituency. You cannot do it if you don't see the world as they do. Fiction can help you on the path to seeing the world in that manner.

The truth can be stranger than fiction. Another great place to learn from the experiences of others is the biography. We can only experience so much in our own lives. We live in a particular time and a particular part of the world. We cannot go back in time, and we may not be able to uproot to live in another part of the world. These experiences are not available to us personally, but they are available to us through the eyes of others.

Reading biographies can allow us to experience the lives of other people and learn from their successes and failures. If you want to learn about perseverance, read about Abraham Lincoln or Thomas Edison. If you want to read about tenacity and adventure Theodore Roosevelt may be your man. Books about events also can be helpful. If you want to learn about project management, read about the construction of the Panama Canal. If you want to see how leaders interact read <u>1920, The Year of the Six Presidents</u>.

Reading about the experiences of people and events will help you by adding to your experiences without having to take the time to live through those experiences. Now, these learned experiences are not necessarily as powerful as lived experiences. We all remember as kids and teenagers that our parents or teachers would tell us that it is a bad idea to do something. They shared their experience with us, but we did not listen, and many times we got the poor result that they told us about. We needed to see it for ourselves. Just reading about it or being told about it won't cut it all the time. Sometimes we need to stick our toes in the water or dive right in. It is not enough to be told about the sun on our face we need to feel it.

In cases where we need to experience something, the biography may inspire us to action. We may never have considered taking a leave of absence to drive across country or to walk the Appalachian Trail, but a book might inspire us to do so. We may not even know that certain experiences exist. We may not know about zip lines through the jungles of Costa Rica or hiking trails in south-east Asia. Reading can open our minds to other opportunities

There are times, however, where the biography will open our minds through the other's experiences. You can learn from and use the experiences of another, and you can actually have an epiphany. You have a lot of experiences. Since you only have your perspective to go off of, you may not see how your experiences connect and how you can use your experiences to get ahead. When you see from the lives of other people, you get a different perspective, and you can see potential in you that you never thought you had.

You should read about people that you like, but also about people you don't like. Politics is a great example. People can feel very strongly about politics. If you are reading about American presidents and you only read about Theodore Roosevelt, Ronald Reagan, and other Republicans but leave out Truman and John F. Kennedy, you are only getting a partial picture. You are not looking at the world from another perspective. If you are partisan, it is even more important for you to read about people from the opposing party. If you don't, you can get blinded by your own feelings.

The same goes for other subjects. If you are going to read about Edison also read about Tesla. If you are going to read about combustion engines also read about steam engines. Read about your religion but also other religions. Expand your horizons. The more perspectives you can see from, the better you can relate to more people. You will have a better understanding of how to work with those people. You will be able to serve them better, and in return, you will be better able to succeed. One of my favorite motivational speakers said the best way to get what you want is to get enough other people what they want. You will only be able to get them what they want if you know what they want. You can better know what they want by understanding them as people. To understand them, you need to be able to see the world through their eyes.

We can all use help with our soft skills, but sometimes we also need to spruce up our hard skills. We need to improve our performance in what we do. A low cost, convenient way to do that is by reading technical books. These books can cover everything from selling, to spreadsheets, to parenting, to raising chickens. Whatever skill you need, there is a book out there on it. When you have an e-reader, there is also a lot of free content available to you.

There are the bestselling books out there, and they are bestselling for a good reason. They offer the most people the information they need. There is also another group of books. With the advent of online shopping, many more books have become available to everyone. This comprehensive marketplace has allowed lesser-known authors to publish their work. The quality of writing can vary, but a lot of times these books are very helpful because they are written by the people who do the work, not professional writers. These books are cheap and plentiful. They are so cost effective that you can get one idea from reading the book and feel good about your investment.

I have a subscription that allows me to "borrow" this class of eBook for a flat monthly fee. The subscription gives me the opportunity to audition books. I can look through it to see if it has what I am looking for then read it in depth. If I don't like the quality of the writing or if it is not exactly what I wanted, I just return it and get another book. This service gives me the freedom to explore books and see what information is out there. This service is very helpful for more obscure subjects.

I train in the martial arts, so self-defense is one of the skills I like to study. There are a lot of books out there on self-defense. Some that teach theory, some that teach techniques. Having access to those books has given me a source of information that we just did not have twenty years ago. It is easy and many times inexpensive to access this information. You just need to look for it.

All these reading strategies take one thing to work. You need to read the books. It can be on an e-reader or a traditional book. Use whatever you feel comfortable with. You are reading this book, so you are showing that you are open to the concept. You need to spend more time doing it. It is time to turn off the TV and read. It is very hard to do that these days. There are so many distractions. It is 5:30 in the morning as I am writing this, and my phone is already buzzing. I need to make a decision. Do I keep writing or do I feed my electronics addiction and check my phone? Since I have committed to writing this book, I left my phone until after I was done. You need to do the same if you want to achieve the results.

If you are going to commit to yourself that you will proceed with a strategy for self-improvement, then you do need to make a commitment. There are things you need to do. You need to work; you need to spend time with your family, you need to take care of your house. There are things you don't need to do. You don't need to watch TV; you don't need to surf the web, you don't need to play games on your phone. You need to decide what you want and what you are willing to give up to get it. If you fill your life with empty activities, you will end up with unsatisfying results.

The traditional learning venue is the classroom. Having a teacher is a great way to learn. There are free classes available online and from certain organizations. We are not all made of money. When we are struggling to put food on the table, it can be hard to justify spending hundreds if not thousands of dollars on classes. Luckily there are a lot of free classes out there on relevant topics.

The main source of free classes available is internet videos. These videos range from tutorials on how to fix a toilet to lectures on advanced physics. These classes can be very helpful. Since they are recorded, you cannot ask the teacher a question, but you can rewind and watch the video over and over until you understand it. These classes are also convenient. You can watch them on the train on your way to work; you can wait until the kids are in bed to watch them. You can watch it for 10 minutes then finish it later. These classes are very flexible.

Taking these classes do miss a few things. As I mentioned before, there is no teacher interaction, so you can't drive down to certain specifics. There is also no student interaction. In a classroom, we tend to learn as much from other students as we do from the teacher. There is also a networking opportunity when there are other students in the class. These videos are valuable. You do learn new things, and they can be a great way to reinvigorate your learning prowess, so when you are ready to take the next step, your mind is in learning mode.

There are free classes in a classroom setting. You need to be a little more careful with this type. Many times, these classes are a means to sell you a product. You can glean information from those types of classes, but those are not the classes that I am talking about. Some organizations provide free education. Banks, for instance, are required to support the communities in which they work. One of the ways they do that is to offer classes to the community for free. There are a lot of organizations that offer job-hunting classes for free and certain clubs offer training in the skillset that they represent.

It takes a little research, but with our good friend Google (or Bing if you prefer) you will be able to find a lot of free classes on a lot of subjects. These classes are helpful and have valuable information but to get a full classroom experience you will need to pay. There are also some very valuable web sources that cost money. These sources can help you get to the next step once you have exhausted the free content or if you are looking for more interaction on a larger variety of subjects or if you need accreditation to get ahead.

The internet is also a great source for learning content. There are paid sites that give you access to teachers online, and there is student interaction as well. We have gotten more and more isolated with our electronic communication. We can video chat with friends from across the nation, and we can text and email for business. The face to face meeting has become a secondary means of communication. The internet has translated to the education sector. There are classes online that are led by teachers and that allow students to interact online.

Colleges offer these classes as do other organizations. Some of these offerings are local, and others are worldwide, so you can select the range of students you want to encounter. The prices can be less than traditional college courses, and you have the opportunity to take the classes in your home. These sources can give you access to schools outside of your area or just give you the convenience of learning from your home. Some of the local ones will have student get-togethers so you can interact with the students offline.

These classes give you the professional teacher interaction that videos and books can't offer. There is value in being able to ask a teacher a question and have them rephrase a concept in a way that makes it more understandable for you. Having a teacher can be especially important if you are taking a class that you have no background in. These classes can be a great way of supplementing your education.

There are organizations that offer training classes that last from an afternoon to a week. These classes are typically career support classes. If you are looking at these classes, you should talk to your company. Even companies that don't have an official education system will allow you to participate in classes and may even pay for a part or all of the class. Taking classes like this helps you in three ways:

1. You get the skills in the class
2. You get to network,
3. This is new, you signal to your employer that you want to learn.

The results we get in much of traditional education provides us with a form of signaling. If you have high grades and a good SAT score in high school, you are signaling to colleges that there is a good chance that you will succeed in their school. If you get a college degree, you are signaling to prospective employers that you have the persistence and determination to follow through and accomplish a goal.

Success is not always about being the most qualified or the smartest. It is about the perceptions your employer has of you. Signals coming from you fuel those perceptions. If you persistently come in late, you are signaling that you do not care about your job as much as you should. If you take on additional responsibilities, you are signaling that you are willing to go the extra mile. If you start going to classes, you are signaling to your employer that you will be more valuable to them in the future.

It is important to get the skills; it is also important that people know you have the skills. You can be the best person for the job, but if people around you don't know it, you will not get to where you want to go. Reading books and taking free video classes help you with skills, but unless you can talk about them at work, they do not help you. Telling people about the classes is signaling to them that you are informed, willing to learn and flexible. Talking about paid classes, especially if you are willing to invest in the tuition yourself, signals that you are willing to commit to your own future and are a valuable asset to your company.

As we discussed earlier in the book, this applies to outside of work as well. If you are a parent and your kids see you doing homework, what do you think will change about their view of homework. You are signaling to your kids that homework is important enough for you to do it and they are more likely to take it seriously. That goes for reading as well. Kids seeing you read will set the example, and they are more likely to read too. The videos may not be that great of an example. They watch too many videos as it is. You are constantly sending off signals to the people around you. Make sure that they are the signals you want to send.

Education is also a signal. The level of education that has become synonymous with the American dream is the college education. There have also been criticisms that it is too expensive and that they don't teach the skills needed to succeed in your career and that there are other paths. Let's expand the college education stage to any post-highschool career development training. It is true that the college degree signals that you are willing to commit to a process and follow through. However, completing a plumbing program and apprenticeship also show commitment to a process and follow through.

Having only a high school diploma without some additional training can be a barrier to entry in many jobs. As we discussed earlier, we want to remove as many barriers and obstacles from our path as possible. Now some people drop out of college with a great idea and pursue it, take risks, and become very successful. If you have one of those ideas, go for it. There is a good chance you will fail the first time, and that is okay. We all make mistakes and experience is the best teacher but to succeed you need to take risks, and they don't all work out the way we want them to.

If you don't have that idea or if you have too many financial obligations right now to start a business, it is time to start to stack the deck in your favor. You don't necessarily need to pursue a college degree. You just need to educate yourself. If you are a toolmaker, take classes in drafting or engineering. If you are an EMT, go for paramedic training. If you are a bookkeeper, go for your associate's degree in accounting. Review the path that you are on and if you like that path, determine what you can do to get you further down that path. Ask yourself if you want to be doing the same thing ten years from now.

Once you start asking yourself those questions, it will be easier to see what path you want to take. It is then you can start planning where you want to go and how you can get there. There is a good chance that you will need to get some kind of training to get to where you want to go and organized post-highschool classes can be a part of that growth.

If you do have a college degree, you may need an advanced degree to set yourself apart from your peers. As you move up the ladder, having an advanced degree can be a prerequisite for some positions. The caliber of school can also matter in some instances. It is a little less common these days, but some companies do reimburse employees for taking college classes. If you are not taking part in those programs, you are leaving money on the table. The class is valuable and if you are willing to commit the time and the company is willing to spend the money then you should take advantage of it. It both signals to your employer that you want to grow, and it puts marketable skills in your pocket at your company's expense.

Constant learning is the key to growth. You need to be able to keep up with technology and to speak intelligently on a multitude of subjects. You also need to be able to speak at the level of your audience. Have you ever been listening to a speaker and they sound either like they are talking to children or they are talking to PhDs in physics. These people are either talking above or below their audiences. You need to be able to recognize your audience whether you are talking to one person or a thousand and gear your message towards them. The only way you can do that is to have a range of experiences that allow you to speak to all those people.

In today's dynamic world we need to wear many hats. Whether we are working or parenting or volunteering, we are required to have a lot more experience than we were in the past. There is so much to know. In parenting 20 – 30 years ago, we did not have to know about social media and the impact it has on our kids. We did not need to know about smartphones or constant access to the internet through wireless communication. These are all things parents now need to know about to be able to guide their children.

In the workplace, jobs are variable. There is more of a contractor mentality than an employer-worker mentality.

Everything seems to be temporary. Jobs change so fast that it can be hard to keep up. Many employers don't even hire many permanent employees. The employees are temporary so that the employer can stay nimble in the marketplace. To survive in that environment, we must be nimble too. These obstacles can make it seem like it is impossible to break out and get ahead, but there are opportunities, we just need to be ready for them.

To be ready to take on new opportunities we need to have the experience. We gain that experience by working every day. To get the extra advantage, we need to supplement that experience with education. Education is what will set you apart from your peers. Getting educated while working is not easy. It is much easier to watch TV or to play softball. Education takes commitment and discipline. You need to work hard at it and spend the time you would normally spend on leisure time. When possible, you should overlap your leisure and education times. This will make the education more satisfying for you.

Take the time and discipline yourself. Set aside a half an hour every day to read. As mentioned above it does not need to be some heavy tome on philosophy. Reading any book will help you. I recommend that you do at least some of your reading when you wake up in the morning. If you wait until bedtime every day, you will find that you only get in 10 to 15 minutes a day before you fall asleep. Also, it is ok to read a couple of books at once. You may spend 10 minutes every morning reading a book that teaches you a skill and then spend 20 minutes a night reading fiction. You can also listen to books in your car while you commute. I do this, and when I had a two-hour commute (each way), the books kept me sane.

If you have not been in a learning environment for a while, start small with classes. Watch some free online videos on a topic in which you are interested. Many of the videos are arranged in 10 minutes to half hour bite sizes, so you do not need to commit half your day to learning. Once you get your learning hat back on, expand to longer classes until you get to the point where you are comfortable with learning again. It can take a while. Learning is a skill just like riding a bike, and it can take a while to knock the rust off. Once you get more proficient, you can expand your learning opportunities without increasing your time commitment too much.

Learning also gives you confidence. As a late bloomer, you have seen your share of discouragement and let downs. You have run up the hill only to slide back down. The knowledge and experience you gain from education are like a rope to help you climb that hill. It gives you the confidence to climb steeper hills and to break out of the discouragement cycle to get where you want to be.

Chapter 7 – Taming Technology

All progress takes place outside the comfort zone.
Michael *John Bobak*

The first step toward success is taken when you refuse to be a captive of the environment in which you first find yourself.
Mark Caine

The one thing that tends to separate the young and the old is comfort with technology. The young are ready to embrace technology, and the old tend to ignore it. Like paying bills online, there are a lot of people my age and older that don't pay their bills online. They mail in checks. Younger people tend to be more tech savvy and take into account new technologies. This is part of the two-edged sword of experience. We know how to write checks better than younger people, but we don't stop to consider if that skill continues to be relevant.

We look for jobs online because the want ads in the paper are gone, but we don't use the online tools to help us find the ideal employer or to help them find us. We wander into technology because it replaces what we had, but we do not embrace it or live on the edge of it and understand it as it develops. Because of this people get left behind. Younger people learn the technology faster and have the appearance of knowing more than the older experienced person. The appearance of ignorance is bad for the older person but also the company.

Technology is the tool, not the experience. I heard a story that demonstrates the point. A shipowner had a problem with one of his engines in his most productive ships. He was losing money every day the ship was not operational. He spent thousands of dollars with multiple mechanics to no avail. Finally, he hired an older very experienced mechanic. Being frustrated over the lack of progress from previous attempts, the owner watched the old man work. The old man looked the whole engine over, he poked at it and prodded it, and finally, he went to his toolbox. He pulled out a small hammer and hit the engine in a specific spot. He then went to start the engine, and it worked.

The owner was very happy. A week later the owner got a bill for $10,000. Having seen the man just hit the engine with a hammer, he asked for an itemized bill. The old man sent a bill back reading. Hitting engine with a hammer $10, Knowing where to hit it $9990. Technology is just a tool. You need to leverage your experience. You need to know technology to help you leverage it and to also signal to your employer that you are aware of the technology out there.

On the flip side, sometimes you need to step back from technology and get to work. Sometimes you need to address a crisis. There is no time to come up with a technological solution. You just need to get the job done. When I was younger, I was an apprentice toolmaker with my uncle. He was (and still is) technologically savvy. He has computerized machines and drafting software. He tries to stay ahead of the curve so that he can remain competitive. One of his customers had a crisis. They had very short production windows, and they damaged one of their molds. Somehow, they put the cutting die in the machine incorrectly and instead of cutting out the part, it came down on the mold and damaged both the die and the mold. Since literally every minute the machine wasn't working the company was losing money, they had to fix the machine fast. The customer brought the damaged parts to my uncle's shop. Did he set up one of his computerized tools? No, we got out welders and grinding disks, and we got to work. In this case, experience won the day. My uncle's experience with working metal allowed us to get the work done much faster manually than any technological solution would take.

You need to know how to use your tools. Just like you would rather use a screwdriver than a hammer to drive in a screw, you want to use the right tool for your job. Just remember that sometimes the power screwdriver does not fit and your experience getting a manual screwdriver up and behind a part that you can't see well is your best solution. If your only experience is technology, you will be lost when that technology fails you. If you realize that the technology is just a tool and your base experience is the driver, you will get far.

On the other hand, if you have the experience but not the technology, you are hammering nails with a rock rather than a hammer. So, a monkey with a hammer looks more experienced than you do even though you may be the only one who knows exactly where to drive that nail.

You don't need to just know about and understand technology; you need to use it. If you understand what a hammer is and how to use it, but you still use a rock to hammer a nail you are still not efficient. You need to keep up with and use technology. You also need to use it appropriately.

Completely setting up a LinkedIn page will help you reach your goals, playing Facebook games probably won't help you reach your goals. Signing up for or writing blogs about your interest points is helpful, mindlessly searching the web is not.

Technology can make you more efficient. There are so many apps out there to help you with your day. There are calendaring and to-do list apps to keep you on track. There are mapping apps that help you get to where you want to go whether you are driving in the suburbs or walking in the city. There are apps to help you find restaurants when you are traveling. There are a lot of apps that can save you time and money and just make life more interesting for you. These tools can help you leverage your skills and get you to the next level.

You don't need to be on the cutting edge. Getting the latest and greatest gadgets can be expensive and not all the technology sticks. You need to stay just ahead of the pack and know how to use the tools you have. If you have the super-duper phone with the watch that is connected and all you do is take phone calls, that is a waste. If you have a standard phone and you can map your way to an appointment, find a good restaurant for lunch, track your appointments and your to-do list you are ahead of the game.

The key is using the technology you have. If you don't have much ancillary income, there are a lot of free options out there. If you can afford it, use the tools that best fit your needs. You need to do some research to see which ones work best for you; then you need to use them. You will not reach your goals by playing games on your phone. You need to be engaged and deliberate in your use of technology.

These tools can be your friends. You can make your life more efficient, so you get more done with the time you have. Every minute you save can be a minute you spend on your goals or leisure. We need to rest occasionally too. Use your technology effectively, and you will be better equipped to achieve your goals.

Even though you don't need to buy all the new tech gadgets, you should keep up with all the trends. It is important to know what is happening in the tech world and how it will affect you. Your job may count on it. If you were a gas lamp lighter or a buggy whip maker at the turn of the 19th century, you most likely found yourself out of a job. In England, there were riots when thousands of needle makers were put out of business by automation. The needle makers were not ready for technological change, and their lifelong skills were made obsolete. You do not want to be obsolete. You need to keep on top of technology.

In America at least, we have put generally less emphasis on manufacturing labor due to the general feeling that we cannot compete. The number of manufacturing jobs has decreased, and a lot of that has to do with technology. It is cheaper labor combined with the technological advancements in other countries and technical advancement in transportation and logistics that allow for the mass importation of goods and now services.

With phone systems on the internet, we can now have people in other countries take our call center jobs. When this first started, there was a backlash because of language barriers. But those barriers can be overcome with training. Even the automated switchboard has improved. Since voice recognition has improved, you don't see people yelling

"YES!" into their phones as much. Technology has improved.

These technological advances typically add value. They reduce costs, make things more efficient and help improve poverty in other countries. It does have local impacts though. If you were the call center manager who lost his job because the company moved, it is a big negative. Even if you did not lose your job, the additional competition reduces your chances for career growth. It is important to understand technical advances. It is not just cheap labor elsewhere. It is the technological advances in transportation to get the products from the countries in which they are produced to the stores in your neighborhood, or the internet phone to bring the representative from halfway around the world to your phone

Technical advances can also create jobs. The energy industry has seen a lot of positive job impact due to technological advances. Renewable energy has created jobs that haven't existed before. Fossil fuel technologies have also created jobs. These advances have hurt jobs in the coal industry, and nuclear power seems to be on a downswing due to lack of safety innovation there. Changes can drive innovation. We will probably see cheaper clean coal technology and safer nuclear that will drive jobs the toward those industries.

Technology can make life generally better, but it can cause local hardship. You need to keep an eye on technology trends to see how it can impact your job. It does not matter what line of work you are in. If you are in security, you need to look at drones. If you are in health services, you need to look at automated life-saving devices like defibrillators. If you are in the fast food industry, you need to look at automated ordering kiosks. The list goes on and on. The travel agent industry was hit hard by the internet. Even garbage collecting has been affected by technology. There used to be three guys and a truck. Now there is one guy with a robotic arm on the truck.

Even if your job or home life are not financially affected, knowing about technology is important. It gives you something to talk about and signals to the person you are talking with that you are relevant. The big joke is the grandkids have to act as IT support for the grandparents. If you are older, you are not expected to understand new technology. If you do, that puts you ahead of the game. It makes you even more useful and relevant. You can leverage your experience and use your knowledge of what is coming to be more strategic and add more value and demonstrate your continued relevance. This experience can allow you to accomplish more and get closer to reaching your goals.

If you can forecast innovation and change your path, you are more likely to be successful. If you were a gas lamp lighter and you thought that electricity was the next big thing and you trained in running wire, you got ahead. If you traded in your buggy making tools for car repair tools, you did OK. The same goes today. If you see technology that will have an impact on your life, positive or negative, you need to get out in front of it, so you control the outcome, and you have a better chance of coming out on top.

Chapter 8 -Position Yourself for Opportunity

The starting point of all achievement is desire.
Napoleon Hill

Logic will get you from A to B. Imagination will take you everywhere.
Albert Einstein

We have always heard that you must be in the right place at the right time to be successful. I believe that this is partially true. Showing up is 80% of success. In "Lotto," you can't win if you don't play and in success you can't win if you are not engaged.

Part of engagement is awareness. You have to be aware of what is going on around you and aware of trends in the industry. In the previous chapter, we discussed that you need to be aware of technological changes. That is not the only thing you need to track. What is happening in your industry and how will that affect the way you proceed? If you are in the mortgage industry and rates are going up, you can no longer rely on refinances as you once did, what do you do to succeed? You are a tool maker at a helicopter plant, and there are cuts to the defense budget, what do you need to do to be successful. It can be like playing a game of chess. You need to think two or three moves ahead.

To do this, you need to leverage all the things we talked about in the previous chapters. We need to be reading and learning. We need to have mentor relationships. We need to employ technology.

The key is to have situational awareness. I am a martial arts instructor along with being a financial services executive. I am always teaching students about situational awareness for self-defense and self-defense is a good metaphor for traversing an uncertain career or parenting or volunteer environment. The only difference is the projected outcome. In self-defense, you are trying to keep you and your loved ones safe. In the others, you are trying to reach the goals you set for yourself without hitting any pitfalls.

Situational awareness is basically knowing what is happening around you at any time. Using the self-defense analogy, you should not be engrossed in your cell phone while you are walking through a dark parking lot. By doing so, you may miss the gang of hooligans in the shadows ready to pounce on you. In the same way, if you are a mortgage originator in an increasing interest rate environment, you should not be distracted by your past success in refinancing mortgages when the interest rates indicate that refinances will decrease, and you will need to find another avenue to continue your success.

Continuing the self-defense analogy, if you are walking down the street and you see a group of teenagers harassing people as they walk, what do you do? Do you walk into them or do you find a way to avoid them? The same goes for your career. If you hear rumblings that your function is at risk of being outsourced or that your company is buying technology that has the potential of making your position obsolete, what do you do? Do you keep doing what you have been, or do you make changes to reduce your risks?

It is always better to have an idea of what is coming so you can react to it. Unfortunately, we do not have crystal balls to tell us the future. We need to make educated guesses on what to do next. This means leveraging our experience. We need to be nimble. Being nimble means, we need to have the pragmatism and energy to do new things. We have to work with other people. Life is a team sport. We cannot go it alone and expect to achieve our full potential. Success is also a numbers game. Being engaged means having a really big tent in which to operate. You need to build your network beyond your immediate environment.

As we position ourselves for success, it is time to start bringing everything we learned together and building our plan.

Where can you find success? A good place to start is your own experience. That experience may only tell you that you are on the wrong path, but that is a start. You have worked at building your life for many years. Whether you have been stuck in the welfare culture, you have been a blue-collar worker, or you have been an executive, your experience tells a story, and you need to listen to it if you want to take advantage of it.

The movies and American culture, in general, have idolized the money makers. Whether they are business people, actors or athletes, success has been measured in money earned not necessarily in the life lived. If money were the object, then the founder of a successful charity cannot be considered successful because that person has not made as much money as a professional athlete.

To me, earnings alone is a poor definition of success. Success is reaching a goal. If a parent wants to give up the material things to raise their children, they can be successful. If an executive is burnt out and starts a restaurant, that person is on a path to their success. I am not a person to say just follow your passion. I am passionate about martial arts. Unfortunately, I have financial and personal obligations that I could not support if I were to dedicate my life to martial arts right now. I train when I can, and I feel good about it. I have other goals that I want to achieve, so I have put training as a lower priority.

"Success? I don't know what that word means. I'm happy. But success, that goes back to what in somebody's eyes success means. For me, success is inner peace. That's a good day for me." Denzel Washington

Your experience is a personal thing. I cannot tell you what your experience is since I have not lived it. You are the only one who has lived your experience. You are the only one who understands it. That is why you need to be cautious of people giving advice. They do not necessarily know your true potential. They have not lived the life that you lived, so their advice may be flawed.

Many people will tell you your faults. Everyone wants to help tell you what you have done wrong and why it means you can't move on. Whatever you did wrong is a lesson. As long as it has taught you something, then you are ahead of the game. If you touch a hot stove and burn yourself, you have gone to a class on how to not burn yourself. If you continue to touch hot stoves and burn yourself, then you have not learned the lesson. On the flip side, if you never touch a cold stove again, you have still not learned the lesson. If you remember that a hot stove will burn you, but a cold stove will not, you have learned a lesson. You have an asset. You are better at managing the stove than you were before.

People may come back to you and say that you are bad at managing the stove because you burned yourself. The opposite is actually true. You are a better manager of the stove. You have firsthand knowledge of what the stove can do, and you are in a better position to train others on using the stove. This may be a silly example, but it demonstrates how mistakes teach and how the lessons you learn will have an impact on your future success.

Mistakes can hurt you in the short run and even hold you back. I told you earlier about my sick day costing me the respect of the president of the company. The fact that I was actually sick did not matter. I learned a lesson that day. When I am responsible for a task, I am responsible. Whether I am sick or stuck in an airport or name another problem that can come up, I am responsible. That was a painful lesson, and it haunted me for a couple of years. Even to this day, there are a couple of people who don't trust me as they did before that day. Does that mean that I can never be sick or have some other problem? No, it means that I need to leverage other resources to make sure the job gets done.

Which sounds better, "I am sorry boss I am sick and can't present at the client meeting in 2 hours" or" I am sorry boss, I am sick, so I am having Marty present at the meeting today. He is prepared, and I am confident he will do a good job."

It would be better for me if I could do it. I am missing an opportunity, but by providing for the meeting, I have fulfilled my responsibility and did not leave my boss in a bad spot.

It is lessons like that one that can pass us by. Being burned by a stove is an easy mistake to identify. Calling in sick when you have the flu may not be. It wasn't an easy lesson for me to see. It took time. As discussed before, I started not getting key assignments, and it put me back a couple of years in my career development. It took time reflecting on my experience to realize the mistake I had made. Reflection on your history is one of the ways your experience can help you.

The things you were successful at and things that make you happy are also keys to use in finding your path. If you are an accountant but find helping people with their careers more satisfying, you may be better in human resources. If you are in corporate America but find more satisfaction in charity work, you may be better off working at a nonprofit. You need to review your experiences and use them to find a path to success. Whether that review results in finding that you are on the right path or the wrong one, you have built a wealth of assets in those experiences. The ideas you have had, the lessons you have learned, the people you have met can all help you in your path. You need to review and document the experiences you have had and take advantage of those assets as you move forward in the achievement of your goals.

You have found your opportunity and identified your goals. Do you have the energy to take advantage of it?

I have been working towards my career goals for many years. I finally feel that I am getting traction, and it is a lot of hard work. It has long hours and a bit of travel involved. I have some family and household responsibilities too, so I always have a lot to do. To do all this work takes energy. I need to get up early, so I can do some of my reading, and I typically had written this book between 4:45 and 6:30 in the morning depending upon my schedule. Then I would put in a 10 to 12 hour day. I would work out when I could and did what had to be done around the house. From my experiments with pushing myself, I found that when I ate badly or went too long between workouts, my energy level would slip, and I would be less effective at accomplishing my goals. Are you up to that challenge or will you be down for the count?

Energy does not last forever. You need to be in a position to recharge when you run low on energy. A motivational speaker I listened to years ago told the story of an accomplished old lumberjack and a younger up and coming lumberjack. Everyone told the younger lumberjack how great, the older lumberjack was. The younger lumberjack felt that he was, the better lumberjack. He was younger and stronger and faster. The older lumberjack never bragged, but the other lumberjacks kept pressing the younger lumberjack about how great the older one was. Finally, the younger lumberjack was frustrated and challenged the older lumberjack to a contest.

The older lumberjack at first declined but then acquiesced. The day was set, and everyone was excited. The two lumberjacks would take their axes into the woods and after a full day, whoever had harvested the most wood was the winner. The day started, and after an hour the young lumberjack noticed that the older one would leave the woods. This made the younger lumberjack feel good. He thought the older man had to go rest after an hour, but the younger man felt he could keep going. This happened every hour that day, and the younger lumberjack got more and more motivated and worked harder and harder.

Finally, the day was over, and the judges counted the logs felled by both competitors. All the men gathered, and the judges proclaimed the winner. The older man had beaten, the younger man by several logs. The younger man was perplexed. He could not understand how the older man could beat him when he took a break every hour.

After dinner, the younger man approached the older man and asked him. How could you beat me when you took breaks every hour? The older man laughed and told the younger man; I did not leave to rest. I left to sharpen my ax.

We need to do that too. We need to make sure our tools are sharp. Staying sharp means that we need to read and learn to keep our minds sharp, but just as importantly, we need to eat right and exercise to keep our bodies sharp. Can we succeed without doing those things? Yes, if we don't, it will be a lot harder and as we have been discussing. Putting self-inflicted obstacles in our way is unproductive. By keeping our minds and bodies sharp, we will have the confidence and energy to achieve our goals. Having this energy at our disposal will keep us ready to accept the challenge of a new opportunity.

When opportunity knocks, you need to be able to open the door. If the job you wanted or the parenting opportunity or the volunteer work you always wanted to accomplish came to you, but you were too out of shape to accomplish it, that is worse than never seeing the opportunity in the first place. Things rarely fall into our laps and when we have an opportunity we need to take it.

Taking advantage of opportunities requires action and action requires energy. That is why most people sit on the sidelines. Lack of energy is the primary reason why after 30 or 40 or 50, people give up their dreams. When people say, they are too old for something, that means that they don't have the energy and they have lost the drive to get that energy.

Now some things would be out of reach. It is unlikely that someone will be an Olympic sprinter at age 50, but that person might complete an obstacle course race. As I have mentioned earlier, I have had people younger than me tell me that they are too old to do what I do. The fact that I am older and do the task means the issue they are experiencing lies elsewhere. Why can't these people do what I do? It isn't that they can't. It is that they won't. They won't eat healthily. They won't work out. They won't wake up early and get more done. They won't make a plan.

There will be some things you can't do. But most of the time you will find that there are things you won't do. If you won't do them, that means you are making a choice. That is good news. If you are making a choice, you have control. If you have control, then you can make changes. If you can make changes, you can get on the path to your goals. It takes discipline and hard work, but you can do it.

There is a reason most people give up on their dreams and settle into a routine. It is easy to give up. It is easy to watch TV and eat processed food. It is easy to go to the same boring job every day. Planning healthy meals and exercise is hard. It is hard to go out and achieve your goals. The hard work has the benefit of the satisfaction of reaching your goals. The easy path ends in regrets and lost dreams.

Be ready for the opportunity. Start now to build the discipline to do the things we discussed in this book. Now that you have the energy and confidence you need to get to where you want to go.

The quote, "No man is an island" is very clichéd, but it is true. It can be very hard to succeed by yourself. You need people around you to succeed, and it helps to have the right people around when you are scouting new opportunities. Many of us have the misconception that a mentor or sponsor is someone who gives you a job. There are very few people who will look at you and say, "we need this person in the organization, and we will pay them lots of money." It doesn't quite work that way, and mentors can exist outside the workplace as well as inside. They are teachers and advisors, not the goose that laid the golden egg.

Since it is unlikely someone is going to hire us out of the blue, how do we identify and execute on opportunities? We have talked about having the knowledge base and having the energy to execute. Now we need the team. What is your support system for finding opportunities? I don't just mean a group of people telling you that you are doing a good job. Who is out there working for you?

"Successful people are always looking for opportunities to help others. Unsuccessful people are always asking, 'What's in it for me?"
Brian Tracy

Support systems are multi-level:

- You have the highest level, the sponsor who provides access to opportunities. The sponsor might be multiple people like a customer base. It can also be a single executive who has a career move to offer.

- There is the mentor; this is a person with more experience than you who you can learn from and can guide you on your path. You can have multiple mentors, one for work, one for parenting, one for hobbies, etc.

- Peers, these are the people on the same level as you. They may have different tasks, but they are the same level generally.

- Last, there are subordinates. These members don't have to be people who report to you. They are just people who have less experience than you that you can mentor or sponsor.

You need to make sure your team has all of these people in it. They each carry a specific perspective that can be valuable to you. Also, remember that this is a team. You need to give as well as take. Expect to help all of these people out as much if not more than they help you out. This team is not like a sports team. The members don't need to work together and may not even know each other. They are a team around you.

This team can communicate different opportunities to you as you are searching, and they can help you take advantage of them. You can fill the need of a sponsor, making their lives easier and in return, you can have a satisfying career change. A mentor might know a person with a need, and in return, you can fill it. You make it possible for a mentor to help a colleague and you get a satisfying career move. You need support in your next move, so you hire peers and subordinates or get them hired in other positions. These are ways of getting your network to work for you. They see that you will help them. You are not just a taker.

Building a support team can work outside of the office too. If you are fundraising for a charity or trying to be a better parent or getting involved in a new hobby, you can leverage the people you know to make the experience more satisfying for you as you make the experience more satisfying for them. Where many people fail is in giving back.

If you take and take and take, you are not a team member. You are a moocher. How many times have you gotten a call or an email from someone you have not talked to in years asking for help with a job search or some other thing. They never checked in to see how you were doing. They never offered help on anything. They just asked you for a job after years of no communication. How does that make you feel?

Not good. Don't be that person. Your team is an asset that you need to nourish. Feed it if you want to harvest from it. It is just like a garden. If you nurture and cultivate it, you can have a rich harvest.

Do you know the right people to help you reach your goals? Do you have the sponsor, mentor, peer and subordinate relationships you need to succeed? If you don't, you need to find them, and you find them through networking. As I eluded to before, networking is not a one-way street. You do not meet people, and then they shower you with pearls of wisdom and gifts of career advances. Networking is about building relationships and helping people reach their goals.

Will everybody you help be able to help you? No, some of them may not even be grateful for the help you've given them, but by helping others, you signal to your network that you are willing to serve your network, not just take from it. This does not mean that you should help moochers and deadbeats. If you know someone is a taker, you have no obligation to help them, but if you do help someone, and they turn out to be a taker, don't feel bad. You did not waste your time. You are building your reputation as a giver.

You will probably spend more time helping your network than you will get helped by it. As you help your network and you get the reputation of being a grateful, active participant in your network, you will see your network bear fruit. It may take a while to build the correct network. The people you need to know may be three separations from your current network. That means you need to navigate through three layers of people, showing that you are a productive network partner to get to the people you need to know.

Networking is a lot of work, and it can be frustrating. That is why most people don't do it. That is also why we get the last-minute cries for help when people lose their jobs. Having the right network has a lot of benefits. You hear about information before your peers. You have access to job listings that most people don't. All those jobs are not meant for you, but you can make introductions. You help someone fill an opening, and you get someone a job. You have helped two people with one action. You have shown yourself to have a valuable network and your willingness to use it to help others. These are valuable assets that can be used to get you what you need from your network, plus you get the satisfaction of helping friends out.

"It is literally true that you can succeed best and quickest by helping others to succeed." Napoleon Hill

As I said before, a good network is like a garden. More than likely you will find a lot of weeds in your garden. That is unavoidable. You need to control them, so they don't overwhelm your fruit-bearing plants. It is the same with your network. You will find that certain unproductive people will try to take all your time. You need to avoid this. It is a trap a lot of networkers fall into. A good example comes from an experience I had a few months ago. I was at a conference with a coworker. We were trying to drum up business for our company. There were a couple of people there who could not add value to the company, and there was no strategic reason to talk to them. They ended up taking a couple of hours of my coworker's time that would have been better spent talking to other people.

Now you shouldn't be rude to these network weeds. Unlike the garden, network weeds can turn into fruit bearing plants over time, but they will suck you dry right now. You do need to control them. My coworker should have spent 15 minutes talking with them and then found a way to extricate himself from the conversation. He then would have had time to talk with people who could have had a more immediate impact on the company.

You need to keep this in mind. Whether you are at a conference or a happy hour, you should watch out for network weeds. Practice pulling out of conversations even if you have to say you need to go to the bathroom. Every interaction you have with people should be strategic. Even if that just means that you don't want your happy hour monopolized by a boring blowhard. Sometimes you need to talk to the blowhard, but you should not feel obligated to do so. You even have to be strategic in your recreation. Otherwise, you will be vulnerable to the whims of other people and that happy hour can end up being a boring waste of time or that conference can turn into an unproductive expense.

"If you don't design your own life plan, chances are you'll fall into someone else's plan. And guess what they have planned for you? Not much." Jim Rohn

Keep your network fresh and well worked. Always add new people to it. Keep in touch with the other members even if it is just to drop them a note on LinkedIn every couple of months. The old adage, it is who you know rather than what you know that gets you ahead, is only slightly inaccurate. It is who knows you. I know Jack Welch. I have met him several times, but I met him in a venue where I am confident that he does not remember me. I cannot rely on Jack Welch as a networking partner as it sits right now. If I want him as a networking partner, I would need to do a lot more work. There are however a lot of senior executives that do know me. They are networking partners. I can help them, and they can help me.

Once you have your goals determined, go out and build the network that will help you best. It will take time, and it can be frustrating, but just as in your garden once you have the weeds under control, you will reap the fruits of your labor.

Chapter 9 – Keep the Faith, Fight to the Finish

Success is just a war of attrition. Sure, there's an element of talent you should probably possess. But if you just stick around long enough, eventually something is going to happen.
Dax Shepard

Would you like me to give you a formula for success? It's quite simple, really: Double your rate of failure. You are thinking of failure as the enemy of success. But it isn't at all. You can be discouraged by failure or you can learn from it, so go ahead and make mistakes. Make all you can. Because remember that's where you will find success.
Thomas J. Watson

Working hard toward a goal so big that you cannot see the point where you accomplish it is difficult. It is easy to get discouraged and lose faith in yourself. We have people all around us, some who love us and want to protect us and others that want to see us fail, pulling us back and we just don't know if we can make it. Being a trailblazer is hard.

Think of yourself as an explorer of old. You have just boarded your sailing vessel for a land that you believe is there, but you have no idea of the storms you will hit or if you will make it. Scary isn't it. Sitting on your couch looks a lot safer, doesn't it? Your family doesn't want you to go because it is dangerous. There are a million reasons/excuses not to do it. Really big goals can be like that, scary. You need to have enough faith in yourself to carry through.

If you are cutting a path that no one has cut before, you don't know if you can succeed. If no one else has done it, there is a chance that you will not be able to do it. A task can be a lot easier if you know that it has been done before. Writing a book has been that trailblazing path for me. I have written hundreds of articles over the years, but until now, I have never succeeded in writing a book. I have always had challenging jobs and sometimes very long commutes. With that schedule, I did not think it was possible to succeed in writing a book. My perspective of a new author was the underemployed writer that wrote all the time waiting for their big break.

It wasn't until I read about Tom Clancy. He had a "real job" when he was writing, and he was able to write a book that put him on the path to greatness in the writing world. If you don't know if someone has accomplished a task, it is the same as believing no one has done it. If you do not believe it can be done, it is near impossible for you to do it. The adage "if you think you can or can't, you are right" is true. It is all up to you.

In Star Wars, The Empire Strikes Back, Luke Skywalker is asked by Yoda to move his spaceship with the Force. Luke tries but he does not believe he can do it, so he fails. Yoda tries to move it and succeeds. Luke's response to the success was that he did not believe it to which Yoda responded, that is why you fail.

Even if you are doing something that no one else in the world has ever succeeded at, you can find examples to follow. If you are an inventor, Edison's overcoming failure in creating the lightbulb is inspiring. If you are a politician or aspiring leader, Abraham Lincoln's life will help you. If you are a teacher, reading about Helen Keller can inspire you to try harder with difficult students.

All this inspiration is all well and good. There is still the nagging sensation that we have missed the boat, that we are too old, we should just go gently into that good night. We need examples of people who succeeded later in life. Thankfully, there are a lot of them. Hopefully, you can find one in your network. Having a living breathing person, you can talk to is a real shot in the arm when it comes to being inspired. Instead of that, there are a lot of famous people who are late bloomers. Here is a brief list. Find the person who inspires you. Read about that person. If you are a visual person, hang their picture on your wall. Stay inspired. Use the trail they blazed to make your journey easier.

- **Stan Lee** was in his 40s when he reinvented Marvel Comics
- **Mary Kay Ash** was 45 years old when she started her cosmetics company
- **Rodney Dangerfield** didn't find success in comedy until he was near 50
- **Julia Child** started to learn about French cooking at 32 and opened a cooking school at 40
- **Ray Kroc** was in his 50s when he found success with McDonald's
- **Laura Ingalls Wilder** published her first book at age 65
- **Harland Sanders** was in his 60s when he founded Kentucky Fried Chicken
- **Anna Mary Robertson Moses** (Grandma Moses) started painting in earnest when she was 78 years old.

We need to find the person who inspires us. There are many people beyond the people on the list who have succeeded later in life. You need to find the one that inspires you. It may not even be a late bloomer that inspires you. Theodore Roosevelt inspires me. He was sickly as a child but made a conscious effort to get himself into shape to be able to live the life he wanted to live. Even though he may not qualify as a late bloomer, I find his life inspirational, and I want to emulate parts of it. I say parts of it because there are things he did that do not fit my values.

When his first wife died, he moved out to his ranch to grieve and work out his feelings. That sounds like a good thing until you find out he left his baby daughter behind to be raised by others. That is not something I would do. I am not saying this to be judgmental. I am saying it to show that a person does not need to be perfect to inspire you. There may only be one task a person does that inspires you. The key is to find an example of success that you can relate to and use to help you blaze your trail.

We should all be our own person and not be the copy of another person. We should seek out our own unique path, but it is ok to emulate others. We have all heard that we can fake it until we make it. There have been times in my career that I had no idea how to execute the tasks I was assigned.

Because I had shown an ability to get things done, I was assigned harder and more foreign tasks. To keep going, I needed to fake it until I made it. I kept calm, stayed inspired and learned the things I needed to learn to get the job done.

We all sometimes have the urge to go it on our own. To not listen to anyone and just do it our way. That can be temporarily satisfying, but it is also a path filled with pitfalls. When blazing a new path, there are a lot of pitfalls. If you have ever hiked in the woods or gone cross-country skiing, you know that it is easier to follow a cut path. Following a path is not always possible. However, if there is a path to your destination that provides the journey that you want to experience, there is no reason to cut a new path. It is okay to find inspiration in the work of others and follow the path they took. You may be doing something no one else has done before, but there is someone out there who has accomplished something that can inspire you on your journey. Let their story help you blaze the trail. Learn from their experiences. There is no reason to reinvent the wheel.

The early bird gets the worm, but the second mouse gets the cheese. It is true that being first counts a lot of the time but following afterward allows you to learn the mistakes of others. There is a story of a man who gave up everything during the gold rush to be a gold miner. He bought a plot of land, and he started digging. He actually found some gold and sold the ore for enough money to buy mining equipment. He was going strong until the vein of gold ended. He searched and searched but could not find more gold. Discouraged he sold the mine and equipment for a fraction of what he paid, and he went home. The guy who bought it hired a geologist and found the vein of gold three feet from where the first guy stopped, and it turned out to be a very productive mine.

This story is usually told as a tale of perseverance. Stick with it, and you will get your gold. To me, it is more of a story about learning from others. The first man went out on his own and did not have all the expertise needed. The second man also lacked expertise, but he got it by hiring an expert. He learned from others. We need to be open to help from others. We need to put our egos aside and learn from others, so we don't repeat their mistakes. We can also follow what they did right and feel inspired by their accomplishments. The key is to talk to and read about people who have succeeded. Learn from their successes and failures and apply those lessons to your life.

Sometimes we need an objective third party to give us advice. The people around us and who care about us have expectations and biases. When you work with or live with people, they get certain expectations of you. They expect you to do certain things, act a certain way and that leads them to picture you in a certain position. Those expectations can lead to being pigeonholed. If your boss sees you as a worker bee, he may not groom you to be a leader. If your kids see you as standoffish, they may treat you differently. If you drink a lot when you are with your buddies, they may not see you as a potential triathlete. Our inner circle may have expectations of us that will make them bad advisors for any life changes we want to make.

That prejudiced advice is why coaches can be very helpful. Whether you are looking to get into shape or get ahead at work, a coach is a useful asset. A coach has expertise in helping people reach their goals. They can teach skills but can also be a sounding board and give advice for specific situations. Over time they get to know you, but they are not closely working with you every day, so they do not get the level of bias that your inner circle gets.

As I mentioned in a story earlier in the book, you can get a bad rap for something you did. One misstep can get you pigeonholed or blackballed. You can also get pigeonholed just by traveling down the wrong path and building up frustration. That frustration will leak out and give people a false impression of your potential.

Most people are not skilled at leading and coaching others. Even if your boss wants to train you to be something better, they probably don't have the skills necessary to accomplish it. There is a good chance they will do more harm than good. One of my first manager's first coaching session with me addressed the importance of scheduling lunch every day, not to meet people, just to eat. (true story) There can also be the fear of the appearance of favoritism and misguided company rules that keep managers from coaching their people.

This means that there are limited opportunities to be coached in the workplace and many of those opportunities will be executed poorly. That's the reason we need a third party to look at us objectively, to not be afraid to tell us about our failings and to have the expertise to help us move forward. Each of our paths is unique. As we discussed earlier in the chapter, there are probably similar stories to ours that we can learn to help us on our journey, but they are not exactly the same.

You have your own cast of characters around you. You have made decisions in your life that have put you on this path. You have your own goals and your own unique starting point. This uniqueness requires a specialized plan.

When looking for a coach, think about what your goals are and what your starting point is. Coaches can be specific. Let's use fitness as an example, if you are looking to improve your running technique, you shouldn't go to a powerlifting coach. If you are looking for general fitness, you probably don't want to go to a specialized coach but a general coach. The same goes for your career. For someone just starting out, a general career coach would be a good idea. It is also a good idea if you are moving into a corporate environment from a non-corporate environment. However, as a late bloomer, you probably already have a lot of experience, so the general coach will not be as helpful to you. You need a specialized coach.

Let's say you are a middle manager, you are tired of the corporate rat race and want to start a business. You have always wanted to open a breakfast shop. You have a goal, open a breakfast shop, and you know where you are now, middle management. How do you make the jump? We all hear that a high percentage of businesses fail each year. Does that mean you shouldn't pursue your goals? No, it means you better have a good idea of what you are getting into and have a plan to get there. Does being a middle manager give you all the skills you need to be a breakfast shop owner? Probably not, when you are a business owner you are responsible for everything, as a middle manager, you are responsible for your little section of the world. As a middle manager, you are also not preparing food and drinks for customers.

A coach specializing in entrepreneurship and restaurants is someone you want to meet. Flipping through the channels on your television you will see shows about people going in to help fix restaurants, bars, and hotels. Although the shows can be overly dramatic, they demonstrate how coaching can help. The coach gives you advise on things you probably haven't thought of. They can also help you with your transition plan. There may even be ways to start your business while you are still working so you can have the benefit of your income while you are getting your business off the ground. They can help you avoid the pitfalls.

The same goes for someone who wants to stay in corporate America. If you are stuck in the doldrums of middle management, an executive coach can help you plan your path to C-suite positions. They can identify your failings and help you make corrections. Due to the biases and expectations mentioned earlier in the book, you may need to leave your current company to start fresh. A coach can give you objective advice on how to proceed.

Coaches can help with things other than careers. Success goes beyond work. Hobbies, families, religious affiliations and other avocations also add to a successful lifestyle. If you are overworked, you may want to go to a life balance coach. If you are not confident in yourself, you can get coaching to help you build the confidence you need. As we mentioned before, there are coaches for fitness. There are also coaches for nutrition. You can find guidance on a myriad of subjects.

Remember too that seeing a coach is not a lifelong commitment. You can have multiple coaches for different things without breaking the bank or spending half of your life in meetings. A coach does not have to be a hired individual. I will use myself as an example. I have an executive coach. I pay him, and he gives me an objective view of what I should do to reach my goals. I go to group martial arts and fitness classes. The teachers coach me outside of class. This coaching can mean talking to me after class for 5 minutes on things I need to improve or private lessons to work on specific techniques. I also go on an annual retreat with my church. There are classes and discussion sessions that help me expand my faith. All of these are coaching. Some cost money; others don't They all have the same purpose, help me achieve my goals.

"Changing our lives to put us in a position to achieve our goals can be like turning the Titanic." CCB

Going after a mentor-mentee relationship can be a little daunting for us. The toughest obstacles we will face building a relationship with a mentor live in our own minds.

- We are afraid of looking foolish or showing weakness.
- We may not feel comfortable sharing our failings with others.
- We can also be stubborn and not want to follow the advice of others
- We may believe we are too old to have a mentor.

This can make us reluctant to enter into the mentor-mentee relationship. The mentor relationship has been portrayed as the older executive taking the new kid under his wing to help him through his career. This perception is not necessarily reflective of reality. The mentor does not even need to be older than you. It can be counterintuitive, but someone in their forties may have more experience than someone in their fifties. Age is not a limiting factor. However, if you are 50, I wouldn't take a 25-year-old as a mentor. The 25-year-old may be able to teach you something, but that is not a mentor relationship. The mentor needs to have an understanding of the path you want to take, and there is too much of a spread between the 25-year-old and the 50-year-old. I get information from 20 somethings all the time, but I do not go to them for advice on life-changing situations. Their experience is too far removed from mine to let them guide my decisions.

I have a spread of mentors that I use. These are not formal "mentor" relationships like some companies try to institute. These are relationships built over the years with people I respect. These are people younger than me, my age and older than me. They have a wide range of experiences, and they can act as sounding boards when I have a problem, and they teach me stuff out of the blue. Most times, it is just talking. They are friendships with the benefit of access to expertise. In response, I am a good friend to them. I have helped them in filling jobs, getting customers and sometimes offering advice of my own.

Avoid arrogance and being stubborn when dealing with younger more experienced people. There are some pretty smart younger people out there, and we can learn from them as much as they can learn from us. Don't close your mind to their knowledge because of their age. You need to stay current on many topics, and there are some topics that younger people have more experience with than we do. The cliché topic is technology. This technology can also include social media. A younger person may be able to help you reinvent your personal brand online or open up a new market to you or integrate technology into your day to day activities to make you more efficient.

You can even return the favor and mentor one of these smart younger people. Always remember, the mentor relationship can be a two-way street. If the mentor can get as much out of it as the mentee, that is a solid relationship.

We have all heard that it is hard to teach an old dog new tricks. As we get older, we get set in our ways. We tend to get less active. We see the benefits of a strong home life and may not want to work long hours. In other words, we change. This change can signal more stability, but it can also signal less pragmatism. We can get to the point where we are almost afraid to try new things. The potential to stagnate is why we need to keep active both mentally and physically. We need to have the stability but not the rigidness that can come by being set in our ways.

There is a lot of inertia that comes with following a path even if it is the wrong one. Changing our lives to put us in a position to achieve our goals can be like turning the Titanic. It can be very hard to do it on our own. That is why we shouldn't try to do it on our own. As we have said before, we have enough obstacles in our path. We don't need to add more because we are stubborn. Coaches and mentors will help us turn our Titanic. The longer we have been on the path, the more we need a coach or mentor because of the inertia we have built up.

We need to realize that having a coach is an investment, not an expense. Since they are typically paid, they have an incentive to help you from the get-go. If you have financial constraints, you may want to start with a mentor relationship. Mentor-based solutions are not quick fix solutions. They take time and effort. If your mentors get the impression that you are just looking for stuff, they will avoid you. You need to build a relationship first, and that takes time. Since the coach is a service provider and they get paid to help you, you don't need to spend time building a relationship first, so the process takes less time.

If you do not recognize the value in using a career coach, you can experiment with non-work activities first. Hire a personal trainer to help you with fitness or a nutritionist to help you with your diet. If you have a hobby or are active in your church, seek out mentors in those communities. Once you see the benefits, you will want to do it more. More than likely once you start looking at it, you will probably find that you have at least one mentor relationship right now even if you don't think of the relationship in those terms.

You need to fight the inertia of "I have always done it this way." The world is changing at a staggering rate. We do not have the luxury of staying on one path as our parents could. Jobs, technology, and influences on our families are all changing faster than ever before. We need to be able to keep up with it if we are going to succeed and not be left behind.

There are moments in history where members of society were left behind. Read about the introduction of pin making machines in England during the industrial revolution to see an extreme example. We are in that type of environment. There is a good chance that people who stick to their path with no considerations of the changes around them can be left behind. There is the idea that when you reach a certain age, it is very hard to find a job. That can be true. If you have isolated yourself from the changes going on around you and have not built the proper relationships, you could be in trouble if you lose your job.

It is really important for you to stay connected both literally and figuratively. Having coaches and mentors can help you choose your path. Being a coach or a mentor for others will expose you to the up and comers who can teach you the trends you need to keep your eyes on to stay relevant. This connection gets to be more important as we get older. We need to fight the tendency to sit back and disconnect. It is a battle for relevance. In my writing, I have used canoeing upriver as an analogy for fitness as we get older. If we stop paddling the river pushes us back downstream. This analogy also fits our career and everything else we work hard for. We paddled upriver to be a good manager, or we paddled upriver to be a good parent, or we paddle upriver to be a good martial artist.

If we slow down, as a manager, we get pushed back down river, and we become less relevant and in turn less valuable to the company and will be more likely to get cut. As a parent, if we slow down as our kids become teenagers, we are not helping them as much when they need us most with all the pitfalls they face today. As a martial artist, if we don't keep up our training, we get pushed back down the river, and our technique suffers, and our discipline loosens. We don't reap the benefits we once did.

Coaches and mentors can't paddle for us, but they do remind us why we are paddling in the first place. They can cheer us on when we are tired. They can tell us to steer to avoid the rapids. They can show us how to paddle more effectively, so it does not take as much effort. No matter how old you are, a coach or mentor will help you get to where you want to go faster than you could get there on your own.

Chapter 10 - Why Do This?

What seems to us as bitter trials are often blessings in disguise.
Oscar Wilde

Twenty years from now you will be more disappointed by the things that you didn't do than by the ones you did do. So throw off the bowlines. Sail away from the safe harbor. Catch the trade winds in your sails. Explore. Dream. Discover.
Mark Twain

Late Bloomer

Why bother with striving to be a late bloomer? Aren't we closer to the end of our path than the beginning? Why should we bother putting forth the effort? One reason is that we are living longer. We have the opportunity to do more things because we have more time to do them. With a better understanding of how the body works, better healthcare and improved sanitation than in the past, we are healthier and can have the opportunity to live longer.

What do you want to do with that time? When Social Security came out people were not living long past 65. They had a couple of years in retirement. Now people are living into their 80s. What would you do with 20 years of retirement? This question is especially relevant if you do not have the money to have a very comfortable lifestyle once you retire. What will you do, watch TV?

This question is an important thing to think about now while you are in your 40s and 50s, even if you are in your 60s. What will you be doing when you are 70, 75, or 80? If it is not sitting around and watching TV, will you be healthy enough to accomplish it? You may be able to function pretty well being very overweight at 50, do you think the same will be true when you are 70?

You need to consider what your life will be like when you are older.

- Will you have the energy to do what you want to do?

- Will you have the money to do what you want to do?

- Will you have the support systems? What do you need to do to make sure you are in good enough physical condition when you get older?

- How can you bolster your income to make sure you will have the money needed to get done what you want to get done?

- Are you spending enough time with your family?

- Are you showing your family that you love them and want to spend time with them now?

When you get older, you will want that interaction more, and it may not be there for you if you don't invest in it now. You need to do an assessment of yourself. You need to be honest, and you need to put together a plan to get to where you want to go.

There is no guarantee that we will have a long healthy life. Any of us can die tomorrow, but we should plan for the eventuality of living longer. No matter how long we live, we should strive for a fulfilling life. What that means is different for each person, but it should be our goal. Life is challenging, but it can be exciting. It becomes dull and frustrating when we help other people reach their goals but do nothing to reach ours. You can reach your goals working for someone else, and you can be trapped accomplishing someone else's goals of being an entrepreneur. You need to make a conscious effort to work on your goals, and you need to make a regular assessment of your progress.

Even though it is never too late to make a change, the sooner you start, the better. Inertia will keep pushing you down the path you are on now. You need to make sure you are on the right path. No one wants to sit down at the end of their lives and say I could have done this or I should have done that.

Think of goals as the oxygen mask on an airplane. You need to put on your mask before you help others. Focusing on your goals is not a selfish act. On the plane, if you pass out from lack of oxygen, you will not be able to help anybody. It is similar with your goals. If you do not work on your goals first, you will begin to resent the people around you, and you will not be able to help them as effectively because you will be distracted by disappointment, regrets, and dissatisfaction.

When this dissatisfaction gets mixed with the set in your ways mentality, you get labeled as the old grumpy person. I know people in their forties who have been labeled as a grump. Being grumpy makes you unpleasant to be around and causes opportunities to slip away from you. There is a good chance that if you let it continue, you will find yourself without a job and having a hard time getting one at the same level.

Staying in the workforce can go beyond just being bored or wanting to work. You may need to work. As a late bloomer, you probably don't have millions in the bank waiting for you to finally end your career live comfortably. You need to consider the possibility that you will outlive your money. Most people don't plan adequately for their retirement. I am guilty of that. There are just so many other expenses that it can be hard to start saving early enough that when you get to your 50s, you have confidence that you will be able to retire in the next 10 + years.

There are fewer organizations that offer pensions and even fewer opportunities to stay at one company long enough to build up enough credits to get that pension. You are on your own when it comes to your retirement. We pay into social security but most likely if you rely on social security your quality of life will decrease dramatically. You need to be able to provide for yourself and your family even when you reach retirement age.

This future need is why you need to invest in your health and energy now. Even if you have a perfect pension or savings, things happen. Pension funds go bankrupt; savings are lost.

You need to be healthy to be able to continue to work if you need to. There is no downside to this plan. If your retirement works out well, you will have more energy to comfortably do what you want to do. Travelling takes energy. Hobbies take energy. Watching grandkids takes energy. If you plan for the eventuality that you will need to work, even if you don't need to work you will be better off.

You may need to work just for your peace of mind. People dream of retirement, doing nothing and relaxing. Unfortunately, that can be more pleasant in dreams than in reality. Doing nothing can be boring. Just doing hobbies and busy work can be unsatisfying. People like to be productive. They like to do things that mean something. They actually like to work. Bringing home a paycheck is satisfying. When that opportunity goes away, it can have a negative effect on self-esteem.

Your quality of life can decrease if you want to work but can't because of your health. You may need to work because you don't have enough money. You may also need to work just for your own peace of mind. You need to invest in yourself now and put into place an exercise plan for your mind and body. The mind can get just as flabby as the body. You need to stay engaged in intellectual pursuits as well as physical.

Many of our capacities decline with age. They decline faster when we don't use them. Our minds and bodies atrophy if we are not active. To continue the analogy of canoeing upriver, as we age we get closer to the rapids. It takes more effort to fight the current, and we get pushed back faster than we did before. We need to fight hard to stay in shape. We need to fight hard to keep our minds sharp. There will come a time when the rapids are stronger than our paddling so that we will get pushed backward. Our job is to delay that if possible. Our job is to stay in condition to keep paddling.

Having the ability to continue reaching our goals is the reason we need to do all the things we talk about in this book. We need to:

- Build a supporting network that we help and in turn, helps us
- Stay in shape to continue having the energy needed to move forward
- Continue to learn through classes, reading and mentor relationships

We will be able to persevere longer and take advantage of opportunities that our peers are too tired or afraid to take on.

The whole premise of being a late bloomer is taking advantage of opportunities later than we were expected; to be successful when our peers have given up. We work harder when others are slowing down. Using work analogies as examples of opportunities, we have all been in places where a younger person moves pass us on the career path. The appearance of being passed over is a signal to most people that they have missed the boat. They see the end, and they stick to what they have always done. They believe that they have given it their all and that they did not make the cut.

This belief stems from a sports mentality. If you were in little league baseball and you were pretty successful, then you played in high school and found out that there are a lot of better players and if you went to college and did not make the baseball team, your baseball career was over. That is not how your career works. You are able to make changes and still keep moving.

You do not need the specific talents that a sport takes to be successful in a career. All career paths are much more diverse than a sports path. You are not limited as you are in sports. You can go off in many different directions, and the definition of success is also different. Success is not always about hitting the most balls or getting the most strikeouts. Your career might be to get the other team to hit more balls. You need to stop limiting your career path by comparing it to making a cut on a sports team. There will be times that you don't make the cut in the short term, but there are plenty of ways to get beyond that.

You will find that most of the obstacles in front of you are self-inflicted. You can be your own worst enemy. I read a book a while ago that talked about ego. It compared ego to the airbag in a car. The ego is there to protect your self-esteem. Like an airbag, it helps you when you crash, keeping the "life crash" from destroying your confidence. However, if our egos are out of control, they become obstacles to our success. Think about trying to drive with your airbag always deployed. You are protected from a crash, but you cannot see the road. You just see the airbag (your ego). You have put an obstacle in your way by relying on your ego to protect you.

How will an out of control ego affect you?

- Ego can keep you from learning from younger people or people that you don't particularly like.
- Ego pushes you to go it alone.
- Ego can keep you from writing plans.
- Ego can keep you from taking classes.
- Ego can make you feel like you don't need to put in the extra effort.
- Ego can also keep you from taking risks.
- Ego is afraid of failure.

If there is a risky plan that has a reasonable chance of success, you may talk yourself out of it for fear of failure. The path you are on now is comfortable. You know your path and have a good idea of what will happen. Trying something new does not have that same level of comfort. You do not know your way around this new path as well as the old. There is a good chance you will make mistakes, and there is a chance you will fail.

We need to reflect honestly on where we are, where we want to go and what we are willing to give up to get there.

- Are you willing to give up 2 hours of sleep every night to wake up early and read, exercise or write a book?
- Are you willing to forgo a steady income to try starting a business?
- Are you willing to miss some of your kids' events to get more production?
- Are you willing to give up watching your favorite TV show to take a class and do homework?
- Are you willing to do what it takes to get ahead, make sacrifices?
- **Do you want to be a late bloomer?**

If you are, you need to imagine a clear picture of why you are doing it. You need to understand the benefits. The perceived benefit of the satisfaction of eating a cookie now is much more powerful than the perceived benefit of being fit and healthy. You really need to see the benefits of being fit and healthy to have the discipline to put the cookie down.

We have heard that money cannot buy happiness. It can, however, buy peace of mind. The key to success, however, is not money. It is happiness. If you can bring happiness to yourself and those around you, you are successful. How you do that is a very personal thing, and even the definition of happiness can be challenged. My point is that success is not all about money, although in our society money is a big part of being able to succeed. Even if your goal is helping the community and you have taken a vow of poverty, money is important to help you serve the community.

In our society, we need resources: shelter, food, water, etc. All those things take money. It is very hard to live off the grid, build your own house, get your own water and hunt/grow your own food. Because of our population and the laws around the use of open space, the opportunity to live off the grid like that is rare. Plus, we don't have the necessary skills to do it, and we are giving up many of the things that keep us healthy longer. Food preservation, refrigeration, healthcare, and medicine all cost money. Then if we want to live beyond the basics of adding in education, leisure time, and luxuries, we need more money.

Not to belabor the point, we need money in our society if we are going to achieve our goals. Whether we use it for ourselves or others, we need it. The key is not to get obsessed with money. Money is like air in our society. If we don't have it and we need it, we panic. If you have ever been underwater too long, you start to get the burning in your lungs and you panic. The same can happen when your bills come in, and you don't have enough to cover them. You can panic.

You need to control your money. That means knowing exactly how much you make and exactly how much you spend. With direct deposit, we tend to go through the motions. We don't check to see that we are getting what we are owed. Mistakes happen. I know someone who had a mistake made on their bonus. He was owed 3,000 dollars more than he received. He caught the mistake and it was corrected. If it is a smaller amount, we might not catch it so easily, and that can accumulate over time.

You also need to check your expenses. Your credit card statements are the first place to check. You may have memberships or subscriptions that you don't use. Unused services are just throwing away money. That is money that can go to paying bills or savings. You should also check your other bills. There are ways to cut costs without having a big impact on your lifestyle.

Life balance is also important. A friend of mine teaches a time management course, and he has some great tips on time management. Basic things like saving your work on your computer. If you work for two hours on your computer and you lose the work because you didn't save it, you lost two hours of your life that you can't get back. The same goes for other parts your life. If you only focus on work and neglect your family, you can lose your family. In the best case, you miss out on family milestones, worst case your family splits and you lose years of investment both emotional and financial.

You need to have a balanced life to be successful. You need to have something you do outside of work. I enjoy martial arts, and I am starting to hike. I am definitely a late bloomer on both of these. Most people train in martial arts when they are younger. I injured myself when I was younger, so I stopped martial arts. I did not start again until I was in my mid-thirties and I didn't get my first black belt until I was in my forties. I am in my late forties now, and I just started challenging hikes.

Part of my late blooming is leisure and family activities. I always tried to be there for my family, but I had to provide for them. I had very time-consuming jobs, and I missed a lot of milestones. I was there for my family but not as much as I could have been. I ran myself ragged and was tired a lot. As in my career, I made mistakes outside of work. I did not spend enough time with non-work items. I was not living a balanced life.

Balanced does not mean fifty-fifty, and it is not a constant. There will be times when work needs to come first so that you can pay your bills. There is also a time when your family needs to come first when there's a crisis or something really special happening. There may also be a time that you need time for you. You need to consider all of these things when you are planning your path to success. Success is not just the destination; it is the path. You need to be satisfied along the way. If you are miserable between short periods of success, you probably don't feel too successful. Not every day is going to be great, but you should have a sense of hope and excitement.

To stay motivated is why it is really important for you to define your success. If the success thrust upon you is a high-stress job that takes you away from the things you want so you can have the big house you don't care about, and you are missing the things you want to do, you are not successful. We need to consider this. As late bloomers, we need to make sure that the money fallacy does not blind us.

As we mentioned, we need money to be successful but how much we need and how we get it is not a fixed item. We don't need to be rich to be successful. We don't all need to work on Wall Street. We don't all need to be a tech entrepreneur. You may want to own a bike shop in your hometown, or you may want to be a manager at your company, or you may want to be a stay at home parent. Achieving any of those things is a success if that is what you are striving for.

My wife and I made the decision that we wanted her to stay home as the kids were growing up. If I do the math, that decision cost us well over a million dollars in 20 years. That is a lot of money. Not having that money does not make us less successful. We have great kids, we have enough money now (not always), and we have excess for some luxuries. We are pretty successful. I have not reached all of my goals, so I am still striving. I am a late bloomer on many things I missed when I was younger.

Chapter 11 – A Never-Ending Journey

Don't be afraid to give up the good to go for the great.

John D. Rockefeller

Keep on going, and the chances are that you will stumble on something, perhaps when you are least expecting it. I never heard of anyone ever stumbling on something sitting down.

Charles F. Kettering

Late Bloomer

The journey to success never needs to end. Your priorities will change over time, and you will have different goals, but there is no reason for you to stop trying to get where you want to go.

- People run marathons when they are seventy.
- Some people work in their 80s and like it.
- People enjoy time with their grandkids and their great grandkids.
- People recover from illness.
- People enjoy life.

If they can do it, you can do it!

To do it, you need to decide what you want to do. Who do you want to be? How do you want to live? Then you need to make a plan to get there. How do you lose the weight? How do you get the C-suite job? How do you raise a family on one income? How do you start over after... Job loss... Divorce... Death of a loved one? The thing you can't do if you want to succeed is stand still.

Remember the river analogy. Life is always pushing us back down river. It may seem at times that we are riding a wave, but that is from our effort or the efforts of others. Success does not just happen. You accomplish it. You do it, or someone around you does it. There are people who ride on the coattails of people. Some of those people are dragged to success. That is the easiest path. If you find a trailblazer, you grab on to their coattails and hang on for dear life.

To use a work analogy, this would be like working for an energetic entrepreneur. This situation is a time where you may need to let go of the ego. If a younger entrepreneur has a fast-growing company, he may need an experienced person to help him out. You as a late bloomer can be a perfect match. You have the experience, but you have not made it yet, so you are less expensive than an established executive. You can fill the gaps in experience for the company and grow with it as the entrepreneur makes progress. This type of opportunity can be very exciting and profitable.

You need to let your ego get over the possibility for failure and the idea of working for someone who may be a lot younger than you. You can have fun, be the oldest person in the company and be successful. Sometimes you need to make the leap. It can be scary, but if you keep doing what you are doing, you will keep getting what you are getting. Remember that you may not need to jump in with both feet. You may be able to start off as a consultant. You can work part-time and keep your day job until you are sure the opportunity is right for you.

No matter how old you get or what condition your life is in, always set goals and have a plan. If you successfully sail around the world, you don't want to crash into the rocks at the last port because you threw away your map. If you have been stuck in the harbor for years, you may find that looking at your map will allow you to get out and sail the ocean.

Goals and plans give purpose.

- Why am I eating more vegetables rather than a greasy cheeseburger? My goal is to lose weight.
- Why am I up at 4:30 in the morning to write? I want to finish my book.

We need to have reasons to do things we don't want to, and it is better for those reasons to be our own. If you work in an environment with forced overtime or very time sensitive deliverables, you have probably given up something for someone else. You worked longer instead of having dinner with your family or playing softball or whatever you want to do. You gave up time for someone else, and that can be very discouraging. When we don't have goals, we tend to focus on other peoples' goals.

Your perspective on what you are doing is also important. When I was younger, I would take holiday hours whenever I could get them. Why? I got paid more on those days. Other people would complain about having to work, and I would offer to cover for them. At the time, I was looking for more cash and I could spend time with my family after work. I was achieving my goal by my working holidays. When I got older my goals changed, and I no longer wanted to work holidays, so I made a conscious decision to get a job with holidays off.

You will not know if you are getting anywhere if you have no map. When I was vacationing with my family, we hiked in a national park. We were used to state parks with trails in loops not long trails to other trails. There were actual milestones on these trails. Stone obelisks that showed the mile count and the trail. We had gotten lost. We walked outside of the area for which I had maps. We hit our milestones, but we had no idea if we were going in the correct direction. Luckily, we ran into someone who pointed us in the right direction. We ended up a couple of miles from our goal but my son, a cross-country runner, ran back to get the car.

That experience is the same experience most of us go through in life. We are plodding along trails, and we celebrate when we hit milestones, but we really have no idea what the milestones mean or even if we are going in the right direction. We do not give ourselves a map; we just start walking. On the hike, we ran low on water which slowed us down and could have been dangerous. The same can happen in your life journey. Instead of not having water at the right time, you may not have the right skill or enough energy.

You need a map for the entire journey. You can't have a goal of being the CFO of a company and then become complacent. If you do, you will get off track. On the hike, we had a map of the area we wanted to walk, but we left that area accidentally. Once you hit a goal, you are leaving the area you mapped out. You are in new territory, and you need a new map. You need to know where you want to go next. Even if your goal is to stay where you are, that is your goal, and you need to understand it. If you do not have staying in your position as part of your plan, you may start to slip and not be as effective as you once were. You may start getting frustrated even though you choose to stay where you are. That can result in your losing what you obtained, and you can have a setback.

You need plans to keep you on track. The best goals are written goals. These can be referred to when you are getting lost. Just like the map in the woods. You may have a mental image of where you want to go, but if you wander off the path a little bit, having a written map makes it a lot easier to get back on track.

Your mind needs as much exercise as your body. We exercise the mind through activities just like the body. In martial arts, there are sets of movements called kata. These katas are activities that involve the mind and body. To execute them properly you need to not only memorize the moves and perform them; you need to understand them. The moves can be very subtle and confusing. It takes a melding of mind and body to execute them. That is one of the reasons that I love kata. You need to think, and you need to move. That is what keeps you sharp. Never stop learning. The only constant in the world is change. You don't need to learn microbiology, but you should keep ahead of trends in technology and developments in and outside your areas of interest. Expanding your horizons is good.

You need to think strategically to remain sharp. Your mind needs to be able to work through problems quickly and efficiently. Thinking quickly does not mean acting impulsively. Sometimes you may need a few days to think about something. That does not mean waiting two days and making a poorly thought out, rushed decision. All the learning and reading is helpful only if you take action based on it. If you read hundreds of books but cannot use the knowledge gained, you only read them for recreation. You need to be able to use the information.

Execution is the key. Going beyond what is expected, getting things done, and getting them done well. You need to keep going. Continuing with our canoeing upriver theme, if you read books on how to row efficiently but continue to slap the water with your oar, you will not get anywhere or worse; you will slide backward. Considering your goals and learning new skills is the first step. You need to put those skills into practice.

Mental activities can be as difficult as physical ones. You cannot go from playing checkers to becoming a chess master. You need to learn new skills then use them. Changing from a game with one type of piece with a set way like checkers to chess that has you using multiple piece types all of which move differently, adds a layer of complexity that takes practice to accomplish. In chess, you can practice outside of competition. You can play against a computer or training partners before you go out and play for real. It is harder to do that in real life. You can't practice a sale campaign before you execute it. There are no do-overs when you are performing surgery.

You need to be ready to play every day. This state of readiness is where your experience comes in. Think of your past as practice for today. You acted or didn't in the past, and that is behind you. It is a practice session for today. That is not to say there are no consequences from your past. If you make big enough mistakes, you will need to correct or atone for them. That is like practice too. Let's use physical practice for this example. If you are a star athlete and are about to compete in the Olympics, you need to be at the top of your game. You practice all the time, and you push yourself. In a practice session a couple of weeks before your competition you tear a cartilage in your knee. What happens? It was just practice, not competition, does it count? Of course, it does. You can be out of the competition or at best have limited ability when you compete.

Think of your life that way. Every day is practice for the next, but those practices have consequences. A mistake in practice can hinder you or put you out of the game entirely. You need to have a plan and manage to that plan. Part of managing that plan is developing the skills you need to accomplish your goals. Developing those skills takes education.

Education does not stop when you get a degree. I hear a lot of people disparage education because they did not use what they learned as they progressed through their careers. The thing is, they learned how to do their job somewhere. If they know how to do their job, and they know that they did not learn it in school, they learned it somewhere. They probably learned it by accident, meaning they did not intentionally seek out the information, they just learned it as they went along.

People can progress by learning without a plan, but they have less of a chance to reach their full potential. Think of the gold mine example we used earlier. The gold vein was three feet away when the guy quit. Learning is the same. A better way of doing what you are doing may be one magazine article or one book away. It may be something that makes you more efficient at work, so you can come home an hour earlier to spend time with your family. It may be something that introduces you to an activity that changes your life. You may find that one paragraph which inspires you to carry on that last hundred steps to the peak of the mountain.

The line "it is hard to teach an old dog new tricks" has some truth to it. Beyond being set in our ways, there will be a time when our minds will start to fail us, just as our bodies will. As late bloomers, we should try to delay that as long as possible. We should try to get as many of our goals accomplished as possible and learn to enjoy the journey. I mentioned earlier that we should look at the past as practice. I did not say we should look at today as practice. Today is the big game. Today counts. We may have an injury from yesterday's practice either literal or metaphorical, so we will need to adapt to those difficulties to move forward but practice is over, and we need to play today.

Think of yourself as an Olympic athlete. You see those athletes compete with injuries all the time. There was an Olympic gymnast that got a gold medal even though she was competing with a broken ankle. Did the competition give her a break or did the judges feel bad for her and go easy on her? No, she gritted through the pain and used all her experience and guts to push through and get the job done.

That gymnast was young, but your level of experience is greater, which gives you an advantage. You have more experiences to pull from in your journey. Many of us have the equivalent of a hangnail, and we are bowing out when people with broken bones are moving forward. This should inspire you to do more. If you continue to learn and to put into practice what you learned, you have the opportunity for greatness.

If you have no mistakes that have long-lasting consequences, congratulations you can perform at your best without support. If you have been fired from your job, you have the equivalent of a muscle injury. You need to treat it and enhance the area of weakness that got you fired, then get back in the game. If you severely damaged your reputation or had to spend time in jail, you have the broken bone. You will have the toughest time, but you can still get the gold medal.

The great thing about life is that it is not a single competition like the Olympics. You get to play again the next day, and you get to improve. If you have had serious setbacks, you can still succeed by refocusing and committing to your own success. I watched as some of my peers appeared to cruise through to the higher levels of management, while I was stuck in the middle. It wasn't until I looked closer and saw the full picture that I understood. I was trying to apply my experiences to understand their successes. I was projecting my accomplishments on them, and it was skewing my picture of why they were succeeding in places I was not. It turned out that many of the people who I thought were successes, were not truly successes when measured against my personal definition of success. Each of those people had a different idea of success, which did not necessarily correspond to my definition of success.

"Success is not a destination, it's a journey." — *Zig Ziglar*

Generally, the people who understood what they wanted from life and strove to achieve the life they wanted were successful to my definition. You need to spend the time to determine what you want and put together a plan of how to get it. Even if it just to go fishing on Saturday. I had a job that was very challenging and had such a long commute that every weekday was a loss socially, recreationally and in getting personal business done. I had so much personal business to do on Saturday that I would never have time to go fishing. I talked about it with friends and family. We always said how we should go. They did, I didn't until I made the changes. I needed to get the time to do the things that make people successful. We weren't put on this planet to make a living; we need to make a life. That is a success. Success is the journey.

I know this seems hard and you are probably asking yourself. Why should you do it? If you don't do it, you will always be a victim of your own inertia and will focus on other people's goals rather than your own. What is the point of going to the gym three times a week and why can't I just have that hamburger and fries? It is a lot easier to sit on the couch in the morning watching the morning TV shows than it is to leave the house especially when it is cold and go work out. It is also a lot easier to get pizza or stop at the burger place on the way home to get dinner. We tend to follow the path of least resistance and following that path builds inertia.

That inertia can lead us to become overweight and out of shape. Being in that condition leads us to have a lack of energy and low stamina. We often blame this on age when it is physical fitness. As we get older, we become more insecure about our age. From 18 to 35 we feel like we can conquer the world. Once we reach 35, if we haven't conquered the world we start to wonder if we screwed up or it's too late. When we have that feeling combined with the lack of energy from being out of shape, we build the concerns of growing old and missing out. That is the path to disappointment and bitterness.

We regret the things we did not do rather than the things we did. Don't get me wrong, everyone has done things they regret but it will be the things that you did not do that will haunt you. We see that in a lot of movies and pop culture. We have the bucket list. All of the things we want to do before we "kick the bucket." That list will become one of two things. It can be a wish list that turns into regret, or it can become a plan that turns into a satisfying life.

Going to an exercise class is probably not on your bucket list, but it should be part of your plan if you want to have the health and stamina to accomplish your list. Are you willing to invest 4% of your day 3 to 4 days a week to exercise? That equates to 3 to 4 hours per week. My guess is that you watch 3 to 4 hours of TV a day. Many people are shocked by that number. Monitor the amount of time that you watch TV every day, and you will surprise yourself. You may find that you ware watching 5 to 6 hours a day. There are the shows in the morning, the news at dinner time, that series you can't miss or the big game at night.

You have extra leisure time that we forget about because we fill it with television. On top of that, how much time do you spend on the internet? Between computers, tablets, and phones we are surrounded by entertainment content 24 – 7.

We have covered a lot of material. Let's connect the dots.

- We are getting older; we have poor diet and exercise, so we feel even older than we are, this makes us frustrated, insecure and upset,
- We do not feel like we have accomplished our goals, and we feel bad about ourselves.
- We are surrounded by entertainment where ever we go. We have music, movies, games, videos, posts, tweets and blogs.
- And we typically follow the path of least resistance.

These feelings and distractions lead to a downward spiral. We are inundated with instant gratification that distracts us from the pain and frustration we feel. We drown ourselves in distraction rather than setting our goals and getting to work. Even now I am realizing that I have the TV on while I am typing this chapter. I have it on mute but why didn't I just turn it off? I am addicted to the constant feed of entertainment too. I want to distract myself from the hard work.

There is the joke about Chinese food. It is delicious, and we love it but, in an hour, we are hungry again. That is what these distractions are. When you have a good workout or go on a hike, have a long run, swim, or bike ride, you feel satisfied. You feel like you have done something. When you watch snippets of movies for an hour on YouTube, you feel good at the moment, but it goes away quickly.

In economics, there is the law of diminishing returns. The more you have an item, the less satisfaction you get from it. For example, if you are really hungry and you have a great hamburger, you derive a lot of pleasure from it, if you have a second one you get a little less satisfaction, a third even less and a fourth may make you sick. The same goes for these distractions. The more we immerse ourselves, the less satisfied we are. Since our minds are not like our stomachs and do not tell us we are full, we need more and more content to derive the same amount of satisfaction. It can become an addiction.

By unplugging and having different experiences that challenge us, we can regain our energy and we will find that we do have time to exercise 4 days a week or more. We will find that we feel better and are not tired at 5:00 in the morning when we eat properly. By having a healthy lifestyle and moderating our information/entertainment intake, we can build the energy we need to achieve our goals.

Our lifestyle choices go beyond achieving goals. We need to feel good about ourselves to be happy. It is hard to feel good about ourselves when we are tired all the time, feel out of shape and maybe yearn for the times when we were younger and more active. It is not empowering to have to unbutton your pants to tie your shoes. It is certainly not empowering to suffer from heart disease or diabetes or any of the other health issues that can be caused by being overweight.

We invest money for our retirement. We also need to invest in our health. What is the point of saving money to travel after you retire if you are too sick and tired to travel? You need to have well-rounded thoughts of success. If you work like crazy for a good retirement, but neglect your health what do you have? We have a lot we want to accomplish. We did not accomplish it yet, and we need time to get it done. To have that time you need to invest in yourself. We talked about investing in your mind. You also have to invest in your body. This investment takes work and planned food consumption. You need to intentionally invest in your body the same way you invest in your 401K. You need your body to carry you through your life.

The whole point of this book is that you are never too old to achieve your goals. You may not be a professional baseball player when you are 50, but there are opportunities to play baseball. You may not be a professional fighter at 60, but you can get a black belt in martial arts. You may not be the president of GE, but you can run your own business.

It is really important to understand the "why" behind a destination. I say destination not goal because the true goal is many times hiding behind the destination. When we understand what we want, we stop being blinded by the destination and focus on the goal. The destination is a distraction. It is the thing excuses are made of. I could have gone to Harvard, but I couldn't afford it. I could have been a star pitcher, but I hurt my shoulder. I could have done this or that. Life throws you curveballs. You did not get to the destination. What goal were you trying to accomplish?

We may all be born equal, but life puts us in different places. We may not have all of the same advantages as others. We may need to work harder than others to get to a certain level. We may not have many paths available to us. We may have made a mistake so egregious that our reputations are really bad. When it comes to achieving goals, we are not on a level playing field, and we just need to deal with it. It is easy to make an excuse and go back to playing on our phone.

The key to success is actually knowing what you want. You have to understand your goal and not be distracted by destinations. When I was in college, I started networking to get a job. I did all the right things. I met people, I learned what I needed to do, and I went on my interviews. Everything was going well until all the banks I met with started going out of business. It was the S&L crisis, and all my work opportunities went out the window. I was stuck scrambling for another job.

I never got into the banking industry, and I have had a lot of bumps in my road to success. The key was that I kept focused on my goal of being successful in my way. At times that was very nebulous. Even just dreaming about being a millionaire while driving in my car. I always knew I could be successful. My path was a wandering one, and over time I learned what success was to me. I learned that it was not always about money, but that money was an important factor. I never stopped learning. I am a voracious reader. I take classes. I have coaches. I have had mentors too. By reading this book, you have shown a desire and a commitment to finding your success. You have probably hit a bunch of bumps in the road and maybe a bit discouraged. Commit to exercising your body and brain. Really understand what you want your goals to be. Learn the skills you need to learn and go out and reach your goals.

Thank you for reading. If you enjoyed this book, please rate this book on Amazon.com

Good Luck on your journey!

It is not too late to succeed!

If you have questions when reading the book, go to www.latebloomerbook.com and submit them. I will be answering questions via YouTube.

37370483R00135

Made in the USA
Middletown, DE
26 February 2019